Praise for *The Book of William*

"[The First Folio's] 386-year history is perfect for Collins' peripatetic narrative style . . . Collins is pleasant company on these journeys through musty and scholarly byways . . . This is great, informative fun." —*Oregonian*

"An entertaining consideration arranged in five acts of the serendipitous social life the [First Folio] has experienced over the four centuries of its existence . . . Writing in a style that is light and casual, Collins makes productive use of a vast body of Shakespeare scholarship." —*Los Angeles Times*

"Exemplary scholar-adventurer writing." —*Kirkus Reviews* (starred)

"Gleefully astonishing . . . Collins provides one of the most enjoyable examples of a most enjoyable genre, the book biography, as he tells the stories of individual Shakespeare first folios, their owners, their uses, and their travels. It's a supremely enlightening journey that Collins' convivial manner makes thoroughly gratifying." —*Booklist*

"[A] delightful literary ramble . . . Full of humor, history and travel, *The Book of William* is an excellent summer read." —*Minneapolis Star Tribune*

"Collins knows his way around a good literary mystery, and knows how to milk the bizarre and wonderful detail . . . [He] pours all of [his] mountainous curiosity and good-hearted wit . . . into *The*

Book of William . . . It would be easy to say that this is a book for bibliophiles, or theater lovers, and it is. But as far as what some of us want out of our summer reading—to get lost, to learn something, to laugh—we'd make the case for this as the perfect beach read."

—*Time Out Chicago*

"[Collins] is passionate, knowledgeable and sassy in bringing this story to glorious life."   —*Publishers Weekly* **(starred review)**

"Smashing . . . [Collins] is an enthusiastic and amusing writer . . . a good companion . . . an adept and committed bibliophile, and in the course of his journey into the history of the Folio's individual copies, he comes to a not-so-startling realization; books outlive even the greatest of us."   —*Palm Beach Post*

"[Collins] has done it again. This history—spanning the globe and 400 years in the life and fortunes of one of the most famous books in the English language—is not the dry province of historians, bibliophiles, and antiquarians . . . Witty, detailed, and highly entertaining, it will be appreciated by fans of Shakespeare, history, or human folly."   —*Library Journal*

The Book of William

*How Shakespeare's First Folio
Conquered the World*

Paul Collins

BLOOMSBURY

New York   Berlin   London

Published by Bloomsbury USA, New York

All papers used by Bloomsbury USA are natural, recyclable products made from
wood grown in well-managed forests. The manufacturing processes conform to the
environmental regulations of the country of origin.

LIBRARY OF CONGRESS CATALOGING-IN-PUBLICATION DATA

Collins, Paul, 1969–
The book of William: how Shakespeare's first folio conquered the world/Paul Collins.
— 1st ed.
p. cm.
ISBN-13: 978-1-59691-195-6 (hardcover)
ISBN-10: 1-59691-195-6 (hardcover)
1. Shakespeare, William, 1564–1616—Bibliography—Folios. 1623.   2. Early printed
books—17th century—Bibliography.   3. Books—History.
I. Title.

Z8813'C65 2009
[PR2888]
016.8223'3—dc22
2009006722

First published by Bloomsbury USA in 2009
This paperback edition published in 2010

Paperback ISBN: 978-1-59691-196-3

1 3 5 7 9 10 8 6 4 2

Design by Rachel Reiss
Typeset by Westchester Book Group
Printed in the United States of America by Worldcolor Fairfield

To That Most Incomparable and Noble Uncle,
Daniel Marc Thomas

CONTENTS

ACT I

SCENE i.   New Bond Street, London   3

SCENE ii. Barbican and Aldersgate, London   9

SCENE iii. St. Paul's Churchyard, London   19

SCENE iv. New Bond Street, London   33

ACT II

SCENE i.   Hampstead Heath, London   59

SCENE ii. Catherine Street, London   72

SCENE iii. 17 Gough Square, London   89

SCENE iv. Staple Inn, High Holborn, London   102

ACT III

SCENE i.   Charing Cross, London   115

SCENE ii. High Halden, Kent   122

SCENE iii. Kensal Green Cemetery, London   132

ACT IV

SCENE i.   East Capitol Street, Washington, D.C.   147

SCENE ii. Folger Shakespeare Library, Washington, D.C.   157

SCENE iii. Level C, Folger Shakespeare Library   169

ACT V

SCENE i.   The Globe Theatre, Shin-Okubo, Shinjuku Ward   181
SCENE ii.   Shinjuku Ward, Tokyo   187
SCENE iii.   Meisei University, Hino, Tokyo   200
SCENE iv.   Shinjuku Metro Promenade, Tokyo   215

Further Readings   221
Acknowledgments   245

ACT I

New Bond Street, London

PRACTICALLY SPEAKING, THIS auction room and its contents are on fire.

But it's the slow burn of old books, a combustion through yellowing and foxing; one so imperceptible that it warms rather than consumes, like a living presence pressed against your skin. Sotheby's on preview day is where they glow the warmest, these heirlooms and attic treasures, these cast-off orphans of royal libraries and county manors: they shake off the years of dust to be cradled in the hands of bibliophiles filing in off New Bond Street. Tomorrow these volumes may be headed to a Norfolk book dealer, a Paris expat's mantel, or to a collector in Tokyo—some to be read voraciously, some to never be opened again, and a few to perish when a candle flame or a tectonic plate goes awry. But today these books are together, intact and readable, and bask in more attention than many of them have seen in centuries.

A book dealer next to me hefts in his palm the leather binding of a 1727 *Works* by John Locke, still bearing faint traces of having survived a fire and a flood; on my other side an elderly lady buries her attentions within the red morocco of Lot 75, a 1683 edition of

The Compleat Servant-Maid; Or, The Young Maiden's Tutor. The first instructions in the book are all about preserving—cherries, roses, walnuts, "apricocks"—marmalade of quince, syrup of violets—everything was so *perishable* then. Curiously, after preserving fruit the book's very next tutorial is in the art of writing: the boiling down and preserving of thoughts.

Over here sits Lot 62, a 1598 black-letter Chaucer still bearing the owner's bookplate of one W. Featherstonehaugh; over there in Lot 142 awaits a soiled, spattered, and rubbed copy of *Dracula* bound in what was once bright yellow cloth—the sort of thing you might find in a garage sale—except that when opened it reveals the scribbled-in date of *18 Nov 1897* and this notation:

With best wishes—Bram Stoker.

But what's really attracting attention is not any one book—not even the pale blue first-edition *Ulysses,* or the unpublished Henry James letter ("Too many notes, too many calling cards, dinners, *women,* above all ... I shall crawl into a hole in the sand")—no, what suddenly gets attention in here is what gets everyone else's attention in the world. Put bibliophiles in a room with the rarest books and watch them drop everything when a guy with a Steadicam comes in.

"'I'll break my staff,'" the reporter paces past me, practicing his lines. "'Bury it certain fathoms in the earth. And, deeper than did ever plummet sound, I'll drown my book.'"

The London crew for the Canadian Broadcasting Corporation tracks Don Murray as he strolls across Sotheby's auction room, with his fellow reporter Piya doubling on handling a furry boom mike and checking audio levels.

"'But this rough magic I here abjure,'" Don declaims again, "'and, when I . . . I . . .' ahem . . . *Damn.*"

The cameraman's happy, anyway: it's impossible to take a bad shot in this room. Every single inch of vertical space is polished wood shelving, and every horizontal inch of that shelving is loaded with handsome volumes lined up like suitors, waiting for an auction tomorrow that will be the greatest in Sotheby's history. Arranged between these wall-to-wall books are long tables for dealers to go riffling through everything from Oscar Wilde's personal correspondence and Sylvia Plath's doodle of a teapot to an 1862 letter from the king of Siam ordering more crates of Needham's patent gin. Within a room the size of a Dairy Queen, there is something on the order of $10 million worth of books and papers lying around.

And there's that one book. *The* book.

"'But this rough magic,'" Don starts again, "'I he . . .' No, no. *No.*"

I glance at the Sotheby's staffers next to me. They've shadowed me ever since the doors opened to their inner sanctum and I tumbled through. In a room filled with middle-aged men in spectacles and dapper linen blazers for the July heat, I'm the one guy who looks most likely to douse himself in lighter fluid and scream gibberish about Freemasons. It can't be helped: an hour ago I was at Heathrow scrambling from a delayed red-eye and past customs, baggage lost, checking my watch all the while—*Preview starts at nine!*—and I look all-night-bender disheveled. So they follow me. *I'd* follow me. But as I do nothing but look at the most suicidally boring books— *Proposal for County Naval Free Schools?*—the two finally, in desperation, fall into conversation.

"Word was that we'd have the *Guardian* chap in again today," one says, though they've had every sort of chap in today—American journalists, British journalists, German journalists, you name it. As if on cue, a Chinese journalist wanders in and looks utterly lost.

"Maybe we'll make the front page."

"No," the first shakes his head. Another eminent artist, it seems, has stolen their thunder this morning: "Syd Barrett."

"Oh?"

"Died."

"*Damn* him."

They go off to rescue the hapless Chinese visitor, and another blue-blazered worthy discreetly stations himself near me as I head over to a bookshelf and pick through Lot 84, a collection of books by the Reverend Thomas Dibdin. I delightedly grab *The Library Companion: Or, The Young Man's Guide and The Old Man's Comfort in the Choice of a Library*. I'm approaching an age where I fall between those two chairs, receiving neither guidance to the young nor the comfort of the old; even so, I leaf contentedly through Dibdin's preface. "A re-action is taking place," he marvels of the London of 1825. "Circulating libraries are enlarged and multiplied. The surplus of wealth, in these 'piping times of peace,' finds vent in the channel of book-purchasing." It still does—but now that surplus is elsewhere, in the oil derricks of Russia and the assembly lines of Japan—and so, one suspects, is the next generation of book collections.

"The present age," Dibdin continues, "is peculiarly an age of bibliopolistic adventure and enterprise . . ."

A hushed commotion stirs next to me: a trio of Sotheby's experts, flanked by a vigilant duo of security guards, gather with nervous energy around a large glass display case little more than an arm's length away. Their necks stiffen and spines straighten as a key clicks in the lock, and heads around the room turn as a pair of specialists gently lift out a book reclining on a velvet pillow, where it luxuriates like a monarch. The book is open to its frontispiece; the staffers scrum around each other, ready to catch the precious treasure should some vaudevillian pratfall occur—if, say, one of them steps on a rake or walks beneath a falling safe. They carry it, in fact, exactly the way one carries a heavy birthday cake. And here's what they don't do: they don't wear gloves. The exquisite sensation of human touch is paradoxically vital to book preservation; wear gloves, and you are liable to misjudge the precise action of turning a leaf, and tear a page. Dirty, sweaty fingers keep these old volumes intact. And so they pass me silently, tensely, with their flushed cheeks and damp hands, and between their suited bodies I catch his engraved face, and the flickering glance of words:

Mr. WILLIAM

SHAKEPSPEARES

COMEDIES,

HISTORIES, &

TRAGE . . .

And then it has moved on.

They shuffle carefully toward the far end of the room, a wall entirely lined with an enormous auction lot of Bibles. Whopping and winsome, sleek leather and aged vellum, they represent an astounding profusion of one book across millennia into endless forms and translations. Yet their multiplicity falls mute before a singular presence. When the phalanx of Sotheby's employees sets down the precious volume on a cloth-draped table in front of the Bibles, all attention turns to a book defined by one edition alone.

A small crowd gathers unwittingly around the strange conjunction of lives clustered at this table: Last year Piya, the woman holding the boom mike, was covering the tsunami in her homeland of Sri Lanka. One of Don Murray's previous postings was covering the war in Afghanistan. The ease of modern travel and the miseries of modern nations create these curious amalgams of horror and grace: a year from now, when Piya or Don is watching some crazed youth waving a Kalashnikov on a dusty road somewhere, they will think—*I was reading a First Folio a year ago.*

Peter Selley, the English-literature expert for Sotheby's—he'll wield the auction gavel at tomorrow's sale—sits down across from them. Suited and sharp, the man is as polished as a marble floor. So, Murray scratches his beard, and then he and the mike both lean in a little—what, he asks, is so special about Shakespeare's First Folio?

"It's the most important work in English literature, and indeed the most important secular work of all time," Selley says flatly.

He motions down to the book between them—a stout, unadorned leather binding, resembling nothing so much as a fine slab of old oak—and explains that it's still in an original seventeenth-century brown calfskin and has all its original pages of text. That's almost unheard of. And yet Folio worship means that their ownership has been followed and recorded for centuries. Alone among printed books, you can trace what happened after they left the publisher—crossing borders, shedding pages, transmigrating into new bindings, burning in grates and drowning in wrecks, or treasured in subterranean vaults. In the Folio lays the fate of any book as it ages and makes it way in the world. It is an Everybook—the epitome of the printed word—and in this copy, those words have been fully and perfectly preserved.

It is priceless, except that tomorrow someone will indeed name a price.

Barbican and Aldersgate, London

THE LUNCHTIME CROWD is pouring out the escalators of the Barbican tube, from Aldersgate accountancies and consultancies: AMERICA'S BEST KEPT HEALTH SECRET! boasts the bagel shop sign over their heads, though this would certainly be news to any American. Beyond the dough hucksters, the building houses a sprawling health club, which for many years was London's largest; children splash down beginner lanes in the pool, adults are crunching abs, and everyone rolls over pilates balls like patient dung beetles. The club and the bagel shop are both part of the Barbican complex that runs for block after block along Aldersgate. It's a transcendentally ugly accordion of black iron topped with fat wattle of rough concrete, an escarpment of hostile Brutalist architecture with no visible entrances. Once these were cobblestone streets of wandering poets and playwrights, and of laboring printers: Shakespeare lived here for a time, as did Milton. But from the look of these buildings and streets today you'd never guess that somewhere in this corner—near that orange juicer, let's say—is where the printing press of William Jaggard once stood.

It is hard to imagine a less likely printer for the Folio.

Jaggard was a veteran of both sides of British publishing, having begun in the 1580s as a bookseller with a stall in the shadow of St. Paul's Cathedral. In those days, and for centuries afterward, the hawkers' stalls and printers' workshop windows lining the courtyard around St. Paul's made it the absolute center of the British book trade. This was by design, as having printers close at hand made it easy for the crown to control the country's literature and thus, it was to be hoped, its thinking—a vital power in a dangerously heretical era of vying Catholic and Protestant ideas. All printers had to clear their works with a government censor. A 1586 decree by Queen Elizabeth also limited the operation of printing presses to London, where she could keep a close eye on them, with just one additional press apiece allowed to Oxford and Cambridge. British publishing was left a stunted and easily bullied industry, so unproductive that a motivated reader could tackle every single new book published each year in Britain—a statement that sounds downright fantastical today.

In this small and unambitious craft, William Jaggard set out to make his mark. His time as a bookstall owner provided him with fine training for understanding the public's appetites, and after opening a print shop in 1595 Jaggard scored a hit with his very first title: *The Booke of Secretes of Albertus Magnus*. It was a veritable recipe book of occult alchemy, and to stay out of trouble with religious authorities, Jaggard resorted to that time-honored subterfuge of selling For Entertainment Purposes Only: "Use this booke for thy recreation (as thou art wont to use the booke of Fortune) for there is assuredly nothing herein promised but to further thy delight." With this nod and a wink, readers were free to follow directions on how to make a candle whose light magically made other men appear headless: "Take an adders' skyn, and auri pigmentum, and greeke pitch of Reuponticum, and the waxe of newe Bees, and the fat or greace of an Asse, and breake them all, and put them in a dull seething pot full of water ... and make a taper." Why you'd *want* a decapitative candle is, alas, not explained. But no matter: the book sold roaringly well and into multiple editions, and Jaggard's business was off and running.

His wily instincts nearly got the better of him when not long afterward he came into possession of a manuscript—perhaps even a single stray sheet—bearing two unpublished sonnets by a popular local playwright. The first sonnet was a perfectly serviceable example of the genre, but the second was another matter altogether: *When my love swears that she is made of truth, I do believe her though I know she lies ...*

In those lines Jaggard heard poetry—and the jingle of coins.

He pondered how to spin his find into financial gain. The author had written the sonnets for a patron several years earlier, when his burgeoning career was on hiatus due to a three-season closure of London theaters by bubonic plague. These sonnets had never been meant for publication and had, indeed, never been registered or sold to any printer. They were, in short, private; and there were but two of them. What possible profit could one turn from such a small find?

To Jaggard, the question was one of calculated risk and shrewd cutting and pasting. By interspersing the two genuine sonnets with three more lyrics lifted from another newly pirated play by the same playwright—lyrics never meant to be separate from the original play, let alone published at all—he could nearly triple his genuine poems at hand. These were, in turn, mixed in with fifteen other poems, stripped of attribution, by other poets who sounded rather similar in style. Leave the verso pages blank, set the margins and flourishes extrawide to stretch the whole thing over thirty-two pages, clap some fancy leather covers on, and you have, just barely, a "book."

And you have, more importantly, a book called *The Passionate Pilgrime: By W. Shakespeare*. It was a farrago that none but William Shakespeare himself and his immediate associates could recognize as substantially fake.

It was a savvy if unethical gambit by Jaggard. A few Shakespeare plays had already been pirated by rogue printers such as John Danter, with little record of any penalty being suffered by the perpetrators. Indeed, when Danter was raided in 1597 and his presses seized in midprinting of a pirated *Romeo and Juliet*, it was not for the play—too trivial a genre to warrant much attention—but because he had been caught also printing a banned Catholic devotional. In any case, Danter and others had been careful to publish Shakespeare's plays without the author's name on them. By 1598, though, Shakespeare's popularity was such that his name would sell more copies, and a pirate hazarded to place it on a title page for the first time, in the very edition of *Love's Labour's Lost* that Jaggard promptly pilfered three lyrics from. Jaggard, then, was simply taking the next logical step: using Shakespeare to sell *other* people's art.

It looked like a smart gamble. Shakespeare does not appear to have bothered interrupting his lucrative theater business to deal with grubby, anonymous rip-offs. But to have a printer parading his *name* before the public—brazenly, just blocks from the playwright's own lodgings, and fastened upon what was primarily the inferior work of other poets—this was just too much.

"The author I knowe [is] much offended with M. Jaggard," wrote a fellow playwright, "(that he altogether unknowne to him) presumed to make so bold with his name."

Jaggard didn't care: he reprinted the book again and again, counted his money, and passed on to a respectable career, even landing a lucrative order from King James as the exclusive printer of copies of the Ten Commandments. By the time Shakespeare died in 1616, Jaggard was already well on his way to publishing both the first full English translation of *The Decameron* and a lavish edition of Sir Walter Raleigh's *History of the World*. But thanks to that early and sordid act of piracy, William Jaggard bears a curious distinction in the otherwise poorly documented and indistinct life of our great playwright. He is the one man in the world that we know Shakespeare disliked.

When the aging actors John Heminge and Henry Condell first walked up this street and into the doorway of William Jaggard's shop—sometime, let us say, in 1617 or 1618, a year or two after their old business partner William Shakespeare had passed on—they found an impressive printing operation at hand. There was Jaggard and his son Isaac supervising two presses and looking over the shoulders of eight or nine journeymen and apprentices. The shop might have been hung with drying pages of one of Jaggard's latest projects, *The Method of Curing Wounds made by Gun-Shot*, a text that bore the extraordinary revelation that bullets were not actually *poisonous*— for those shot before this corrective tome had scalding oil poured over their trauma wounds to cauterize the presumed "poison." Or Heminge and Condell might have found apprentices inking the press for pages of another curious project, the *Table Alphabeticall of English Words*. But they'd have found a shop that was both seasoned and not terribly busy—for while Jaggard had tackled complex and ambitious volumes in his prime, ill health had afflicted him for some years. His son Isaac was stepping in more for his father now, though, and the old man himself sounded increasingly confident in public. The shop was regaining its strength—ready to reestablish itself and take on a risky project. Here on this corner, then, was exactly what the pair of old actors needed: a press that was well staffed, experienced, and just a little hungry.

True, there was that old matter of the piracy. That was years ago, though, and even as the spring of 1617 brightened over London, one John Shakespeare was finishing an apprenticeship in Jaggard's shop. The name is uncommon enough that he might well have been a young relative of the late William and helped mend relations between the printer and the family. In any case, the actors had not come to stir up old quarrels, but to do new business. And they could not be too picky about it, either—for if history was any guide, their own time was starting to run out.

Heminge and Condell were what you might call the last two men in a literary tontine. When William Shakespeare died in 1616, his will included a proviso directing "to my fellows John Hemings, Richard Burbage, and Henry Condell, 26 s. 8 d. a piece to buy them rings." Of the six actors who had joined Shakespeare as business partners in the Globe Theatre and its King's Men acting company, these "fellows" were the three remaining survivors.

Burbage would be dead before the decade was out. That left Heminge and Condell as the last two men with a truly intimate knowledge of Shakespeare's plays. The two knew Shakespeare as nobody has known him ever since—not as an artistic icon, but as a friend and a colleague. They'd walked the boards with the man himself, stared into his eyes as they spoke the lines that he had written for them. They'd toiled alongside Shakespeare to maintain the physical structure of the theater, to make payroll, to act in his dramas; together they had seen the awful glow of fire upon the sky as their Globe Theatre burned down in 1613, and when the ashes were cleared away, they had watched the new theater rise in its place. And if the acting profession has not changed too much in four hundred years—

and it hasn't—they'd all had a few too many drinks together at the
Mermaid and wandered home through the darkened streets of London together, their hilarity echoing off the darkened buildings.

Though paired by fate as the last two survivors of the King's Men,
John and Henry proved admirably well matched. Heminge was the
pragmatic businessman of the two: originally apprenticed in the
grocer's trade, the old actor still kept busy managing the Globe,
tending to his London real estate holdings, and operating his own
grocer's shop. Along with Shakespeare, he'd been a shareholder from
the very beginning of the Globe's existence, and he also appears to
have owned the building next door. In fact, for the last decade he and
Condell had been larger shareholders in the company than Shakespeare himself. In Globe financial documents Heminge's name typically comes first, as the one who naturally came to mind when
matters of money arose. He could be quite hardheaded when it
suited him, even going so far as to sue his own daughter-in-law for
his late son's share in the Globe.

And yet there is a pathos to the man. He is described by one ac-
quaintance as "Stuttering Heminge," a detail that may sound non-
sensical in describing a veteran actor. But the stage has long offered a
strange sort of sanctuary to stutterers; reciting lines and singing lyrics
require different mental faculties than conversation does. A stuttering or taciturn man in the world at large may step through a stage
door and turn mellifluous—and in the lines of his friend William,
perhaps Heminge found an eloquent voice to express the depths of
humanity that he himself could not.

Alongside the pragmatic Heminge, there was Condell: an actor's
actor, often remembered kindly in the wills of his fellow thespians.
Condell had come late to serving as a Globe shareholder, content-
ing himself initially with simply pursuing his craft there. After all,

not all actors in the company were business partners. But Condell was wealthy in experience, having acted not only in Shakespeare's plays, but also in at least four Ben Jonson plays. In time, even Condell became well-to-do, taking shares in the King's Men beginning in 1608, and acquiring a country estate and a prime bit of property just off the Strand. Yet he still served his art: Condell trod the boards even now, years after his friend Heminge had slowed down to attend to business concerns.

But they were all having to slow down a bit. Heminge and Condell lived in an age when a fever could bear an otherwise healthy man into the grave in a single weekend. A sense of mortality came easily, given their own time among the memorials and the graves—both men were now churchwardens at St. Mary Aldermanbury—and they were getting old and respectable. Their generation was passing, and with it would pass knowledge of their friend William. And who would preserve his memory then? To the future, Shakespeare might have been duly forgotten as a perfectly unremarkable man: just another industrious quill-scratcher writing cheap entertainments in one of the backwater languages of Europe.

Shakespeare's written record is as nearly thoroughly demolished as this old block along Aldersgate. Of handwriting *unequivocally* known to be his, the words may be counted on your fingers: there are precisely ten. And, in fact, they are but five repetitions of the same two words: *William Shakespeare. William Shakespeare. William Shakespeare. William Shakespeare. William Shakespeare.*

That's it.

Imagine your own life, everything you've ever written—every letter, every grocery list, every school paper, every tax return and receipt and love letter and Post-it note and numb-fingered word upon a foggy window—imagine all of that being crumpled down to a name, to that single line of tangible existence. His signature appears on a purchase deed for a house in London, on March 10, 1611, and once again the next day on the mortgage deed. It shows up three more times in 1616, once apiece on each sheet of his three-page will. Each instance is from the final years of his life, just as he stopped writing plays. Of his artistic prime, a few tantalizing possibilities exist among marginal notes in a manuscript for the play *Thomas More*, but not a scrap remains with any certainty.

Scholars have puzzled for centuries over this simple question: why was Shakespeare so extraordinarily negligent of his own work? How could a man throw everything he'd done into the abyss like that and not leave his own manuscripts behind?

Scholars wonder at this; but not, I think, working writers. Anyone who must live off their words—and I mean *live* off them, in fear of life and landlord from one story to the next—is by necessity unsentimental about their old work. The stuff rather piles up. After a few years you don't even feel much kinship to it: you have moved on to the next book, the next play, the next story, the next fee, the next month's rent. An artist must keep his *momentum*, his ability to move on to the next profitable work. Shakespeare had a family to support and a business to run, and his business just happened to involve a great deal of writing—writing that, apparently, nobody much bothered to save.

In fact, for many plays from Shakespeare's era, only the names survive. Plays neither interested nor rewarded publishers: a play was an event, and the money was in the staging, in the receipts at the door. On a good night, the Globe Theatre could handle an audience of three thousand, paying anywhere from a penny to a sixpence, and would have taken in far more than the paltry two pounds the King's

Men stood to earn from permanently selling a play manuscript to a publisher. Shakespeare and his company didn't fuss much over the preservation or publication of his plays for the simple reason that it was scarcely worth their time.

If we have little preserved in Shakespeare's hand today, the situation in his own time was only somewhat better. When Heminge and Condell set out to print their old friend's plays, they simply had to make do with what they could find; and what they found, it seems, was the typical scattered mess of a busy artist. It had been a decade since William's last play, and perhaps a dozen rough drafts still existed in Shakespeare's own hand. About another dozen revised "prompt book" copies survived from the Globe—it's prompters that flustered actors yell "Line!" to, and prompt books belie their origin by having particularly detailed stage directions that come a little *early*, the better to warn the actors to get ready. Still another dozen or so plays had been published in cheap (and often illicit) quarto editions. With plays like *King Lear*, the best Heminge and Condell could do was to track down these old copies in bookstores and compare what they found with their fading memories of having performed alongside Shakespeare in the plays. Altogether it was better than nothing, but nor was it an entirely satisfactory set of papers to be taking into Jaggard's print shop.

They faced another problem, too: their printer had gone blind.

St. Paul's Churchyard, London

A BLIND PRINTER, surprisingly, was hardly the greatest of Heminge and Condell's worries.

Their greater challenge lay here—in this stretch of St. Paul's Churchyard, now curiously empty and quiet in the afternoon sun. In front of me stands the modern structure of Paternoster House, and through its plate-glass, ground-floor frontage for the Dion Champagne & Wine Bar, an inadvertent dumb show is occurring: two florid old gents, prosperous in their golden cuff links and silk club ties, ostentatiously puff cigars and blow smoke heavenward. They are sitting in the shadow of St Paul's; the darkness is ancient, but the restaurant is sleek and new. Most of the churchyard's old boundaries are overrun by these snug modern streets and sensible brick buildings, with lots given over to a NatWest branch, a travel agency, and a Marks & Spencer food shop full of Ribena and cheese-and-pickle sandwiches.

It was not always this way. The old St. Paul's spire used to be the highest in all of Britain, and it threw its shadow unbroken across a much wider swath of this neighborhood, where sly vendors earned a quick shilling and where government proclamations were traditionally read out to roaring and rowdy crowds. St. Paul's Churchyard freely mixed the holy and the profane: during Elizabeth's reign, a cash-poor government treasury even drummed up funds by holding ten-shilling lotteries in a shed by the cathedral's west door, where they raffled off clanking suits of armor as prizes. Few took much notice that gambling was happening in the entrance to England's holiest site, since butcher boys and colliers already nonchalantly used the interior of the cathedral as a shortcut, wielding coal sacks and bloody joints of meat while sauntering through the west door and then out the east side. Illegal shanties and stalls mildewed out in the churchyard, and shabby and piratical books skulked about the perimeter. Quality was not always their strong point; once, a visiting bishop hurriedly bought a cheap Bible from a stall on the way into the cathedral, ascended the steps to the pulpit, and opened the volume before the waiting congregation to discover that the verse he was to preach on wasn't even in it.

This is where two aging actors would have walked past an entire neighborhood of busy printers, a marked contrast to the underused shop they'd visited in Aldersgate. It was no accident that Jaggard had not quite been working to capacity that decade. The printer had lost his sight by 1612—syphilis being the favored cause for such calamities in those days—so that just as Shakespeare left the stage forever, Jaggard lost the ability to ever see another play. Jaggard still stubbornly ran his shop, though, while allowing his capable son Isaac to step into an increasingly prominent role.

So perhaps a blind pirate would do for printing the works of Shakespeare. The printer was only one part of the publication process: while Jaggard handled the physical task of making marks on paper, a bookseller had the stall or shop to sell it, and the publisher was simply the printer himself or any enterprising fellow willing to

pay a printer to take a job on. Notably absent from the process was
the author. The theater company, not the playwright, owned the play,
and they could sell the manuscripts to whomever they liked; those
subsequent owners were protected, if rather weakly in practice, by
then registering their ownership with the Stationer's Company. The
result was that over the years, Shakespeare's plays had become scattered among at least ten printers and booksellers around London—
most situated in this very churchyard, and operating under, over, or
next to one of the yard's innumerable taverns. In many cases they'd
previously published the slim, cheap quarto-size editions of individual plays, which is why the first buyers of *A Merchant of Venice* were
sent in search of the Green Dragon tavern; find that, tightly packed
between the Three Pigeons tavern on right side and the Rose pub on
the left, and you'd find the printer. The Fox pub was where you went
for *Richard III*. A quest for the Fleur de Lis, cheekily built directly
against the walls of St. Paul's itself, would have led you to the first
printer of *The Merry Wives of Windsor*.

Jaggard was admirably situated to call in some favors from this
motley bunch. Thomas Pavier, the owner of *Henry V* and two other
plays, was an old pirating crony; the owner of *Hamlet*, John Smethwick, was an old business partner to William's brother John. For
those who held many rights, or particularly desirable ones, Jaggard
hit upon a unique strategy: he offered them a piece of the action in
a Shakespeare syndicate. Smethwick parlayed his three coveted
plays (*Love's Labour's Lost*, *Romeo and Juliet*, *Hamlet*) into a partner-
ship, while a local old-timer in the publishing business, William
Aspley, turned in his ownership of *Much Ado About Nothing* and *2
Henry IV* for a place at the table. When one more fellow joined the
syndicate—Edward Blount, a veteran of the St. Paul's trade and already known for such ventures as the first English edition of *Don*

Quixote—it became financially viable. The whole printing trade was so small that around St. Paul's Churchyard everyone knew everyone else anyway—in fact, Blount and Aspley had shops on either side of the same pub, the Angel.

The other play owners would take some haggling. *Richard II*, *Richard III*, and *1 Henry IV* were among Shakespeare's most popular titles back then, and getting them took more persuasion than a sleeper like *Cymbeline*. But a few plays needed no wooing at all. At least three had become derelict; that is, abandoned for many years by their former owners. At first glance, the derelict works are not much of a surprise. There's *King John*, a play from William's apprenticeship that scarcely rouses enthusiasm even among Shakespeare scholars. Then there's the gory *Titus Andronicus*, an early tragedy that sends more eyes than heads rolling. But the third orphan really is a shocker: *A Midsummer's Night Dream*. It may be one of Shakespeare's most frequently performed plays now, but it's a mark of the vagaries of theatrical fashion that Puck and Titania couldn't get themselves arrested in the 1620s.

What was also notable was whom Heminge and Condell *didn't* ask. Opportunistic printers—like Jaggard himself—had published any sort of vaguely believable stuff under Shakespeare's name. During Shakespeare's lifetime you could chuckle over "his" 1605 play *The London Prodigal*—a comedy featuring the misadventures of a pair of servants named Daffidill and Artichoake—or you could peruse "his" foulmouthed *Sir John Oldcastle* ("My Lorde Herberts man's a shitten knave . . .")—or you could gawk at the homicidal father ("Whore, give me that boy!") in "his" true-crime drama *The Yorkshire Tragedy*. You could do all these things and enjoy it heartily; but, despite what their title pages said, you wouldn't be reading Shakespeare.

Condell and Heminge, the last surviving original King's Men, were the only two people left who were qualified to make this distinction, or to judge a line to be truly or falsely rendered. A play's absence from the Folio might be open to any number of meanings—that it was a fake like *The London Prodigal*, that the owner was a holdout as with *Pericles* and *Cardenio*, or that the manuscript was already lost, as seems to have happened with *Love's Labour's Wonne*. So the reasons for absences were many, but the reason for a play's presence was singular. Any play these two men *did* print would be unshakable evidence, a last bulwark against the obliterations of time: here is the man, they said, and here is his play.

A Shakespeare Folio has two irreducible elements—namely, Shakespeare and folio-size paper—and while Heminge and Condell secured the former, Jaggard faced no small decision in choosing the latter. A folio is roughly the size of a modern encyclopedia; or least *was* until the print encyclopedias themselves became quaint. A folio might instead be described as the size of a large phone book, except that those are also becoming obsolete. So let us say this, then: a folio is just the right size for a kitchen cutting board.

The household metaphor is apt, for the paper itself originated in the bedrooms and dining tables of Europe. Be it a Bible or a jestbook, when you read paper of this era you are in fact holding the rearranged fibers of a thousand handkerchiefs, blouses, table linens, and undergarments of everyone from milkmaids to kings. It is rag paper, made from castoffs gathered across Europe from the rudest cottage doors and the finest mansions alike. Worn-out clothes and linens were baled up and sent to Normandy, where a "mistress of the rag-room" would oversee the tearing out of seams and buttons; the loads were then cleaned and bleached in vats of boiling water and quicklime, and after dissolution into fibrous soup they could then be laid and set into a wonderfully durable paper. There were, loosely speaking, five classes of paper—ranging from #1 London Superfine to #5 Coarse Canvas—and each variety of cloth and castoff had its uses. Old, fine table linens went into Superfine paper, while old bits of tarred rope and country woolens went into the kind of harsh paper suitable for, say, wrapping up a ream of Superfine.

Jaggard chose medium-quality rag-paper for printing the plays, which left at least one commentator grumbling later that Shakespeare had apparently warranted "farre better paper than most Octavo or Quarto Bibles." The more provocative decision, though, was the size of the pages. Paper arriving from the mills in Normandy did not come in many sizes, and the size of a book was instead determined by how many times you folded that raw paper over: a Folio took one fold down the center, rather like a modern tabloid newspaper; a quarto was folded twice over into fourths, an octavo folded three times into eighths, and so forth; these folded sheets were then stitched together into quires. The folding created the uncut paper edges that one still finds in old books; and the quires are why, when the book falls apart, pages will sometimes detach themselves in bunches of sixteen, twenty-four, or thirty-two.

For Shakespeare, Jaggard hit upon the sensible solution of once-folded folio pages stitched together "in sixes"—that is, three large sheets folded once, creating six double-sided pages, or twelve numbered sides in all. This meant that the outer sheet of a "six" would contain pages 1 and 12 on one side, and pages 2 and 11 on the reverse. Since he could only print one side-pair at a time, this meant some headache-inducing guesswork for the printer. Clicking on a Print Preview command, alas, was still four centuries away; and while setting up page 1 was simple enough, the printer also had to guess what text page 12 would need to begin with—or, indeed, whether they even *had* twelve pages worth of text to typeset. As his printing of a quire progressed by working toward the middle, the printer could reach the final pairing of pages of 6 and 7 and realize that he had less than two pages of text left to put there. Far worse, though, was to have *more* than two pages left—whereupon the desperate print-shop laborers would nearly run the remaining text right off the page, or shove two lines of dialogue side by side, or just hack entire lines out of the text and hope that nobody would notice. Even so, the pages of a folio were of such a generous size that it was easier to hide such errors.

But then as now, publishing had an unspoken sumptuary code in which certain sizes, fonts, and papers implied certain genres. For folios that meant a work of reference, theology, or highly regarded ancient authors. Other titles took smaller sizes. Take, for instance, *Markham's Maister-Peece*—a 1616 horse-care manual whose advice for securing your steed's loyalty includes fasting him for a couple of days and then smearing honey and oatmeal all over your sweaty chest. Advice like that succeeded so smashingly that within a year the Stationer's Company made the author pledge "That I Gervase Markham of London gent Do promise hereafter Never to write any more book or bookes to be printed, of the Deseases or cures of any Cattle, as Horse, Oxe, Cowe, Sheepe, Swine and Goates &c."

Markham was *not* printed in folio.

To print a work in folio implied a certain gravity, a confidence in the greatness of one's subject. For mere poets and playwrights to use a folio was unheard of, with one crucial exception. In 1616, Shakespeare's friend Ben Jonson had published his own *Workes of Benjamin Jonson*—and had the temerity to do so in folio and while still alive. Though poked at the time for vanity at puffing mere theater into Work ("Pray tell me Ben, where doth the mystery lurke / What others call a play you call a worke," needled one anonymous poet in 1640), Jonson's bold act signaled a fundamental change in how authors understood their profession. In compiling his *Workes*, Jonson created an author's edition to his own liking—not to that of his company, his printer, or whoever happened to own his manuscripts. Jonson believed he had at least some inalienable claim to his artistic creations. In fact, authors did not have any special right over their own works, and would not until the Statute of Anne in 1709 created the first recognizable notion of copyright in English. What Europeans today know as the "moral right" of the artist—a right to not see work altered, adapted, or abused even by those who have bought it—simply did not exist. But Jonson was already asserting his rights, and using his book's introduction to mock his plagiarists and pirates. Jonson was the first playwright to pronounce his plays as art, as *his* art, and as *nobody else's* art.

The great mass of boiled and dissolved linens from Normandy that made their way, cut and sized, to William Jaggard's print house were to go to an almost equally audacious project. Jonson's *Workes*, after all, contained his plays, his epigrams, and a tangle of other writings. But who would be so foolhardy as to build an entire folio around mere penny theatrical entertainments?

"The complaints I hear of thee are grievous," warns Prince Hal.

"S'blood, my Lord, they are false," roars Falstaff.

Or that's what *1 Henry IV*'s jolly old scamp *did* yell when John Heminge played him onstage in 1600; and that is what Shakespeare wrote in his manuscript. It is not, however, what Heminge gave to William Jaggard to print some twenty-odd years later. The second line received by the blind printer in his shop reads, "I'faith, my Lord, they are false."

Something had changed in the last two decades—and it wasn't just the word *S'blood* to *I'faith*. In 1605, King James had passed what was for Shakespeare a rather inconvenient act:

> It is enacted, that if, at any time or times, any person or persons, do or shall, in any Stage-Play, Interlude, Shew, May-Game, or Pageant, jestingly or prophanely, speak or use the holy name of God, or of Jesus Christ, or of the Holy Ghost, or of the Trinity, which are not be spoken but with fear and reverence, *he or she shall forfeit for every such offence Ten Pounds.*

And so it was that London's mightiest wits had the fear of God put into them—or, at least, the fear of ten pounds. Consider that Falstaff is the most blasphemous character ever to grace the Globe's stage— he bellows *S'blood* eight times in *1 Henry IV, and* he turns up in two more plays—and you realize that the profane old lush could have single-handedly bankrupted Jaggard and half the booksellers in this churchyard. It was not a risk to be trifled with. This very patch of the courtyard was once used for a mass book-burning, when chagrined Lutherans were made to torch their own print runs. As it was, every book had to pass through a censor's office before it could even be en-tered as a published work with the Stationer's Guild—and strictly speaking, *all* published books had to be approved by either the Arch-bishop of Canterbury or the Bishop of London.

So out came the *God's blood.* Out, too, came a great many *O God*s and *Mary*s. But the plays gained a couple of words, too: *act*s and *scene*s. At least, they gained what we think of as acts and scenes, thanks to later editors. Look at what Jaggard printed, though, and you find instead the revived Latin terms *actus* and *scaena*—a Renaissance homage to classical playwrights like Terence. The *actus* divisions were inserted by Condell and Heminge; although we may now find it impossible to conceive of Shakespeare's plays as having anything other than the archetypal five-act structure, there's no particular evidence that he conceived of them this way. Scenes are the meaningful units of drama, because they're where physical alterations in the stage are required—props have to be changed, backdrops altered.

By adding to the plays breaks that resemble chapters—and creating an abundance of points at which a reader might set the text down and pause—Heminge and Condell transmuted handwritten actor's sheaves into typeset literature. They transformed a couple of hours of dialogue at the Globe Theatre into something that could be read for days or even weeks, and read alone—miles from any stage, hemispheres away from London, and centuries apart from their own lives and times.

I see them one after another, plastered across the side of #4 Metroline buses roaring past St. Paul's and up Cheapside, bound for Waterloo Station—WE'VE GOT THE GREATEST WRITERS boasts the ad along the entire side of the bus. The ad's inescapable, running on small panels up and down the escalators from the Barbican and St. Paul's tube stations. When you see that balding crown, the thin mustache and hint of a goatee—that oddly shaped white collar that seems to hold the head aloft, as if on a shovel—you immediately know who you're looking at. The *Daily Telegraph* cheekily replaced the face with that of celebrity footballer and sports columnist Des Lynam, but the iconic old engraving will always symbolize just one man: Shakespeare.

The portrait is the one that Jaggard, Heminge, and Condell hired from a local engraver, Martin Droeshout. It is a perfectly service-able engraving for the period. It is also the only *confirmed* portrait we have of Shakespeare—the only surviving picture to have actu-ally been created at the behest and approval of those who knew William. Our entire image of Shakespeare comes through the eyes of Droeshout: every portrait since has been supposition or simply a gloss upon Martin's original vision. For centuries it has been the fashion to mock the portrait as clumsy, presumably by those who wish a Shakespeare that rises from the elements with all nature bowing before him, like a Botticelli on the half shell. What idol-aters are stuck with, instead, is Shakespeare *as he was*: namely, the kind of mustachioed businessman who might have warranted a thirty-shilling engraving job.

To excuse this inconvenient fact, it was assumed until recently that the portrait was executed by Martin Droeshout the Younger, who was but fifteen or sixteen when Shakespeare died; and, well, what could one expect from an inexperienced youth? But *another* Martin Droeshout was working the St. Paul's yard—an uncle, Martin the Elder, who was also an engraver, and who was almost precisely the same age as Shakespeare himself. Given that those collecting Shake-speare's works had been the playwright's old friends and peers from back in the day, the choice of Martin the Elder was perfectly logical. Not only were they pleased by Martin's portrait, Shakespeare's fellow playwright Ben Jonson even went to the trouble of praising it in a poem on the page facing the portrait: "O, could he but have drawne his wit / As well in brasse, as he hath hit / His face; the Print would then surpasse / All, that was ever writ in brasse."

Finding plaudits for William was not hard. All one really had to do was walk over here, just out of the churchyard to the old corner of Bread Street and Cheapside, and enter the Mermaid Tavern to find Shakespeare's old friends. In fact, Ben Jonson offered up not one but two dedicatory poems, a fitting tribute from the only surviving theatrical titan of a generation that had once also counted Fletcher and the ill-fated Marlowe among them. Heminge and Condell themselves included in the volume both a letter to their patrons and a notice addressed "To the Great Variety of Readers"; another poem apiece came from translators James Mabbe, Leonard Digges, and playwright Hugh Holland, all of whom were far-traveled and well-connected Oxford scholars and habitués of the Mermaid.

"He was not of an age, but for all time!" proclaims Jonson, while Holland laments, "Those hands, which you so clapt, go now, and wring / You Britaenes brave, for done now are Shakespeares days." Digges muses, "This Booke, / When Brasse and Marble fade, shall make thee looke / Fresh to all Ages," while Mabbe rather alarmingly comments on William's progress "From the Worlds-Stage, to the Graves-Trying-roome." Heminge and Condell, practical theater men that they are, simply address the reader outright: "The fate of all Bookes depends upon your capacities: and not of your heads alone, but of your purses. Well! It is now publique, & you will stand for your priviledges wee know: to read, and censure. Do so, but buy it first . . . What ever you do, buy. Censure will not drive a Trade."

It is easy to censure or simply overlook *their* contribution, to leaf past these pages in our impatience to read the plays. But what these friends were writing about was indeed the *man*. To see the commendatory verses in a book as nothing more than a sort of obligatory throat-clearing is to not grant Shakespeare's peers the same depth of emotion as we feel ourselves to possess today. Each line is a testimony—not to what we flatter ourselves about being able to judge of his talent or life—but actual living testimony to Shakespeare's humanity and friendship. Even humble Digges, little known now save for his verse honoring Shakespeare, had been a neighbor of the playwright's; his family had overseen the signing of William's final will.

Nor was praise to be taken for granted. St. Paul's habitués knew the cautionary tale of Thomas Coryate; back in 1611, the travel writer haunted churchyard taverns pestering every writer in sight for blurbs, until—in a moment of cruel genius—his victims hatched a plan to pour outrageous praise upon him until his book nearly caved in under the absurd weight of it all. Ben Jonson supervised the pile-on, which included Inigo Jones and John Donne among the pranksters; when it was done, Coryate's 1611 *Crudities* was prefaced by a staggering 108 pages of mock-heroic praise from every corner of this churchyard. The unfortunate Coryate seems to have not even read them before they went to the printer; the very first words of "praise," from Ben Jonson, describe the seasick traveler puking directly into the mouths of fish in the English Channel: "The Author here glutteth Sea, Haddock & Whiting . . . With Spuing, and after the world with his writing." Barfing was a popular theme in the verses, running second only to idiocy, but somewhat ahead of mentions of Coryate's diminutive stature, poor hygiene, and excess body hair. Others noted that they'd never even met Coryate or read his book before being asked for blurbs, and that "Our Author will not let me rest, he says / Till I write somewhat in his labours praises." For this persistence, Coryate was enshrined for posterity in his own book as "an Idiote" and "The Man . . . Whose *Braine-Pan* hath more *Pan* than *Braine*."

The praise for Shakespeare, though, is all more heartfelt for never having been solicited by the author—"he not having," notes their dedication, "the fate, common with some, to be exequutor to his owne writings." If St. Paul's Churchyard could produce shoddy books and merriment at the expense of some writers, it could also take a tender interest in plays abandoned by their own creator. "We have but collected them," Heminge and Condell wrote, "and done an office to the dead, to procure his Orphanes, Guardians."

And orphans are indeed what these plays were. These two old actors, trudging their way through the rain as they made the rounds of London printers and taverns, might have thought themselves performing the final service due to an old friend, and a worthy task to a fine playwright. But it was something more than that. Of the thirty-six plays they gathered in these waning days of King James, eighteen had never before been published. They would most certainly have been lost otherwise: most plays were. Examine the 1592–1603 journals of theater producer Philip Henslowe, for instance, and of the 280 plays he mentions, just 37 found their way into print; the other 243 were lost, with nothing remaining but a title.

Without Heminge and Condell, Mark Antony would neither praise nor bury, for we would have no *Julius Caesar*; and as *Twelfth Night* would never arrive, none would be born to greatness, nor achieve it, nor have it thrust upon them. *Macbeth*, *The Tempest*, *The Taming of the Shrew*, and *The Comedy of Errors* would be mere words—and all the world would not be a stage.

It would be as if the greatest works of English literature had never happened.

SCENE iv.

New Bond Street, London

If you went over to Gordon Square right now, you'd find everything looking rather standoffish. Cyclone fencing is up around the central garden for renovation, while across the street six-foot-high cast-iron spikes surround the Dr. Williams Library. Look up past anti-G8 posters and the adhesion scabs of countless past protests, up the library's neo-Gothic brickwork, and you see gargoyles looking down: lions, men, and lion-men. A few have their faces smashed off. They are guarding the place—but not, it seems, guarding it quite well enough. For there's a gap in the bookshelves of the Dr. Williams Library—a gap a few inches wide and thirteen inches high—and the Shakespeare Folio that it contained for the last 307 years is now before me, here in the rooms of Sotheby's on New Bond Street.

"This is the most important rare-book sale we've been involved with," auctioneer Peter Selley explains to me. "There's been a lengthy process involved. It took over a year. They had an agent who approached two auction houses, and . . . solicitations were made."

The library's motives for selling were not too difficult to divine.

"This single volume," Selley says flatly, "is one third of the value of their entire library."

The journey from Gordon Square to New Bond Street should be simple—go down Tottenham Court, hang a right on Oxford Circus, then a left—but the book's route has been a complicated one. Before it came to this glass case where it reclines royally on a pillow, the Folio took a round-the-world jaunt to woo prospective buyers. In Chicago, a rival curator from the Newberry Library compared its merits to their own Folio: the Newberry Folio boasted a better title page, but Selley just smiled and revealed his copy's most beloved feature—an ancient adolescent notation scratched into the margins of *Hamlet*:

> *Best I desier the readeres mougth to kiss the wrighterres arse.*

"We then took it to Hong Kong and Beijing," Selley says, "where it was wonderfully received. In Beijing all the young people came out—they'd read his works and were just delighted to see the book." It was the first Folio to come to the country; one attendee described it as among the happiest days of his life.

"That market has exploded in the past few years," Selley muses of China. "The auction houses there have had exponential growth."

So has Sotheby's itself on this particular morning: within minutes of the doors' opening, the book auction room filled up. It's not a particularly large room—you could lecture a class of grad students in here—but with folding chairs and standing room only, about a hundred attendees have crammed in. The back of the room is occupied by a riser with a bank of TV cameras, and press photographers wield gigantically goggle-eyed lenses. The buyers are clearly unused to such attention. It is not in the nature of a book auction, you understand.

To understand the world's top book auction it helps to stumble into, say, the world's top *art* auction. Last summer I wandered around

Rockefeller Center looking haplessly for a Christie's art auction until I saw a man stepping out of a limo who *precisely* resembled the top-hatted capitalist in a Monopoly game. So I followed him. We came to a salesroom large enough to seat a legislature in, with screens displaying bids in every denomination of wealth; a gallery of agents took phone orders, and billionaires hid in a series of skyboxes. To gain entry and a little white bidding paddle required a bank statement bearing evidence of sufficient funds. It was only my press pass that got me within spitballing distance of Steve Martin, and I ducked sharp-edged women who cut through the crowd like shark fins. "One million and . . . twenty thousand?" an auctioneer smiled with incredulity, when some yokel dared to raise a Koons bid by a paltry twenty grand. "It's late in the evening, why not? For you, sir, one million *twenty thousand*!"—and the Christie's crowd snickered. It *was* funny—yes, after watching a Rothko go for $22.4 million, that bid *was* funny.

But a book auction is not like that.

Book auctions attract a much higher proportion of men with hair growing out of their ears. They forget where they laid their auction program, and they mutter; they squint and rub their spectacles with a dirty handkerchief; they do not have personal assistants. The book salesroom is truly open to the public, and as disreputable as I looked during the preview yesterday—straight off the red-eye, baggage missing, rumpled T-shirt, and uncombed hair—I was able to handle any book lot I wished. And even now, as the room fills up with studious men in summer linen jackets, the books remain on their shelves around the room, marked off by lot numbers. If you have the nerve, you can pick up and read them even as their preceding lots are getting sold off.

With, of course, one important exception. There, in a glass case at the front of the auction room, stares the portrait page of an opened Folio—the calm and sleepy-eyed man, awakened from a shelved slumber of three centuries—waiting to be informed of where he will journey next.

Even before there was a Folio, there was Folio hype.

If you were a book dealer in the 1600s, your most important clients were generally noblemen, clergy, scholars, and combinations thereof. And for the dealers, one event in all of Europe truly demanded their attendance: Frankfurt. Today Frankfurt is where agents haggle foreign rights with editors amid vast fluorescent-lit trade floors of booths and the faintly sweet smell of slick catalogs. Replace all that with shanties and stonework, cobbled streets and leaning-in timbered buildings, cart horses and lantern-lit taverns, and you begin to get the Frankfurter Buchmesse as it existed in Jaggard's day. Book fairs are recorded back to at least 1473 in the city, for the city's burghers were the original business-minded tourist board; by keeping levies low and zealously prosecuting any crimes against visitors, Frankfurt fostered an international mercantile extravaganza. Books held a special and lofty place amid all the haggling— it is no coincidence that the *messe* of *Buchmesse* also denotes a church mass. And it was a place of learning; scholars from across Europe wandered the streets, and some could even be heard lecturing from booksellers' booths. The book dealers themselves would be absorbed in the guide to newly published titles, the *Mess Katalog*.

It was only after decades of dealers stumbling through half-learned German that John Bill—an enterprising London bookseller and personal buyer for King Charles—put the first English-language edition into dealers' hands, bearing the prosaic title *Catalogue of such Bookes as have beene published, and (by authoritie) printed in English, since the last Vernal Mart, which was in April 1622 till this present October 1622.*

It also bore this curious entry:

> *Playes written by Mr William Shakespeare, all in one volume,*
> *printed by Isaack Jaggard, in fol.*

Curious because it was a folio of plays; curiouser because the printer listed was Isaac and not his ailing father, William; and curiouser still because, despite the catalog's title, Jaggard hadn't actually finished *printing* the book.

This entry—the first printed mention anywhere of the Shakespeare Folio—surely sent at least one or two dealers on wild-goose chases through Frankfurt's streets for a book that lacked the desirable characteristic of actually *existing*. Announcing yet-unfinished books as "published" was a favorite trick of German publishers in the *Mess Katalog*, a way of testing the market, and it seems Jaggard had learned a thing or two from his Teutonic counterparts. The Folio, such as it was, was still sheaves of paper in the Barbican printing house, where work had fitfully progressed between other print jobs and delays at procuring permissions. Some of the folio was printed in the fall of 1621; more was printed the following year; and more still would be printed at the last minute before it was finally registered on November 8, 1623, a full year after it had been announced as "published" in Bill's catalog.

It was then that Isaac Jaggard sauntered down to the Stationer's Hall off St. Paul's Churchyard to witness an entry into the register:

> Mr Blounte Isaak Jaggard. Entered for their Copie under
> the hands of Mr Doctor Worral and Mr Cole—warden Mr

William Shakspeers Comedyes Histories, and Tragedyes soe manie of the said Copes as are not formerly entered to other men, vizt.

Comedyes.

The Tempest.

The two gentlemen of Verona.

Measure for Measure.

The Comedy of Errors.

As you Like it.

All's well that ends well.

Twelft night.

The winters tale.

Histories.

The thirde parte of Henry the sixt.

Henry the eight.

Coriolanus.

Timon of Athens.

Julius Caesar.

Tragedies.

Mackbeth.

Anthonie and Cleopatra.

Cymbeline.

The sleepy state of English publishing might be guessed by the fact that, after making this entry on a Wednesday, the Stationer didn't make another until Saturday. That's when Nathaniel Newbury showed up to register *A Sweet Potrie for Gods Saiunts to Smell on Contryminge Manie Sweete and Choise Flowers*—a collection which has gained rather less fame than Jaggard's more conventional entry. Other Stationer entries like *High-Heeled Shoes for Dwarfs in Holinesse* have not quite found literary immortality; neither has *The Spiritual Mustard Pot to Make the Soul Sneeze with Devotion*, nor *A Shot Aimed At The Devil's Hind-Quarters Through the Tube of the Cannon of the Covenant.*

So the book's existence was now official: with this birth announcement, its sale to the public could begin. And yet it must have been strange for Isaac Jaggard to witness the entry into the Stationer's books: for although his father's name appeared on the Folio's title page, he wasn't here for this occasion. William Jaggard had died just a few weeks earlier.

The blind old printer never did see his unwitting masterwork make its first known sale. Going into London to watch some plays and do a bit of shopping, one Sir Edward Dering of Kent scratched into his account book for the day a twopence purchase of candles, ten shillings for a "per of boothose," and his great splurge of the afternoon: two copies of "Shakespear's playes." For these, he paid the princely sum of exactly one pound apiece.

"The first lot has been withdrawn," the auctioneer announces, and there's a hushed commotion of murmurs and rustling sales catalogs as everyone looks to see what got nixed. It's a 1548 letter by King Edward VI, estimated at a healthy £10,000. Perhaps the owner had second thoughts; perhaps the ownership was contested—or perhaps some fool ripped it during the auction preview—or perhaps it was stolen—or perhaps, perhaps, perhaps. There is no saying. But it's an unnerving way to start.

The first couple dozen lots are all letters and journals, and in their sale you can detect the ascent and descent of reputations: those figures who loom larger in our minds today sell accordingly. History is about the past and the dead, but the *sale* of history is all about the present and the living. The heroes of the present wax while the heroes of the past wane.

"10,000?" Selley calls out. "10,000 to my left. 10,500?"

Standing by his side is a young assistant, a boy dressed in a blue Sotheby's apron, and he's holding the 1851 journal of Elliott Gilbert up for display; a second assistant, a young woman, retrieves volumes from shelves around the auction room as each lot comes up for bidding. The effect of their aprons is to make the lots resemble smoked hams ready for slicing.

"10,500 to the gentleman in the corner. 11,000?"

Gilbert, a navy lieutenant sent to intercept slavers after Britain outlawed the practice, rockets upward to a staggering £16,800, more than three times its catalog estimate. The study of slave history today shines brightly upon his old notebook. Dr. Livingston, meanwhile, can no longer be presumed: one of his letters barely makes its minimum. Handwritten notes by musty English kings of yore—Charles II, James VI, William III—not only fail to make their low estimates, they don't even reach the four figures. You can buy a James II letter for less than it costs to get your VW's transmission fixed. Yet letters from Phrabat Somdet Phra Pormen Maha Mongkut, the monarch immortalized to our era through *The King and I*, roar upward in price. For one king of Siam, you can buy a half dozen crummy old English monarchs.

The book lots fare much the same. A set of early Burns, Donne, and Walton barely scrapes in over its £800 minimum; but women's books—*The Compleat Servant-Maid* and a hand-corrected authoress's copy of a 1765 Elizabeth Griffith play—both leap upward into thousands of pounds.

Dibdin's *Bibliomania* lot, bless his heart, still hits triple its estimate.

But it's Lot 94 that briefly steals the scene—an unpublished 1672 handwritten manuscript by one Dorothy Calthorpe, a diarist and poet writing in "her booke Given me by my Uncell Nicholas." Her scrawled doodles and endearingly big looping letters make the manuscript resemble a Restoration-era Big Chief notebook— but to our time, this common old notebook bound in speckled calf suddenly feels new, fresh, and the rarest of rarities—women's writing that has survived from the 1600s. It soars up and up from its £8000 estimate, up past every previous single item's price this morning, up past the Chaucer and the musty monarchs and the grave old reverends, until it finally alights upon the high perch of £31,200.

A momentary silence descends upon the room.

"Lot number ninety-five," Selley announces.

There once was no "First" Folio: it might have been the Only Folio, as nobody knew if it would sell. The curious new volume was simply *Mr William Shakespeares Comedies, Histories, Tragedies. Published according to the True Originall Copies.*

Shakespeare's graven image on that title page, now staring out over the Sotheby's crowd, has gazed upon Londoners before—it was, in fact, driven through with nails by them and then abandoned to the wind and the rain. Once Jaggard and his assistants returned from registering their book at the Stationer's Hall, they took extra copies of Folio title pages and nailed them to posts around St. Paul's. This is the eminently practical reasoning behind old title pages—their ludicrously prosaic subtitles make sense when doubling as posters. The promise of True Originall Copies, a little ragged and fluttering from churchyard posts in the miserable weather of November 1623, began drawing in customers.

The names of the earliest Folio owners can barely be made out today; they exist in ancient expense books, in estate sale records, and on the flyleaves of the old Folios themselves. A Folio turns up in the library of Sir Thomas Hervey, an MP and a distant ancestor of Nathaniel Hawthorne's. Another Folio endpaper reveals the inscription of *J. Tonstall*—that is, Sir John Tonstall, the queen's gentleman-usher. The old courtier might well have seen Shakespeare's plays acted by the playwright himself—Shakespeare's company was, after all, under royal patronage—and 1623 was the first year in which Sir John began to draw a pension. Walking the streets of London near his home on Silver Street, perhaps he settled upon a familiar old name and the memory of past plays to while away the time. He'd certainly need a good thick book or two—his retirement lasted twenty-seven years.

Publisher Henry Shepherd bought one; he might have been seen perusing it at his shop on Chancery Lane, where he'd later print an edition of Shakespeare's old colleague Francis Beaumont. And women numbered among the early owners—including Rachel Paule, who was both the wife of Charles II's chaplain and the bookish granddaughter of the lord mayor of London. The Folio had respectable sales to respectable customers, and it took no more than seven or eight years to sell an entire run of probably around 750 copies.

Most appear to have stayed in London, but others slowly made their way to points more distant. Scholars still puzzle over one copy signed *Robert Wynn Bodescalion*—who was this Mr. Bodescalion? Ah, but there is no Mr. Bodescalion: there is *Robert Wynn of Bodys-gallen*, a wealthy importer who began building the finest manor in

Wales in 1620. By the time the shelving went up in Bodysgallen Hall, a First Folio would have been waiting for him at London's bookstalls. At one pound per copy, to most householders the Folio represented the cost of forty-four loaves of bread, or perhaps four iron warming pans; but then, the Folio wasn't meant for those sorts of houses.

Students did not buy it; players and producers did not buy it; commoners did not buy that kind of book. For them, sixpenny one-offs of the plays sufficed. But a prosperous fellow like Robert Wynn needed stout, impressive volumes for Bodysgallen Hall's library—and to do that, he probably didn't buy a book, but rather unbound pages. Status volumes like folios were not simply bought prebound off the pile like today's books; they were often sent raw to the customer's own binder to create another brick for the impressive wall of identically custom-bound volumes expected in a fashionable fellow's library. Buyers could eschew the standard calf boards for a sumptuous custom binding with the family arms stamped into it—an extravagance costing the weighty sum of five shillings. Whether the book was ever actually read was not a question to ask of a gentleman. What was important was that he had it and paid well for it.

"The starting bid is one million six hundred thousand."

Peter Selley looks over the crowd as his assistant closes the Folio shut, takes it out of its glass case, and holds it up clutched in her hands.

"One million seven hundred thousand."

Bids are ping-ponging rapidly from a back corner of the room, just feet away from me.

"One million eight hundred thousand . . . One million nine hundred thousand . . . Two million." The heat is literally rising; scholars and newsmen are fanning themselves with the auction programs.

"Two million one hundred thousand . . . Two million two hundred thousand . . ."

Unnoticed in all the fuss, a studious-looking young man in corduroy and elbow patches has slipped into the back of the room, just a few feet to my side. He's a latecomer and looks as if he may have cut out early from school.

And then—this kid next to me *nods his head and bids.*

I look around momentarily—the old fear of being mistaken for a bidder, that staple of sitcoms—and edge away as Selley swings into focus.

"Two million five hundred thousand . . . Two million six hundred thousand?"

The question hangs in the air of the room, and Selley leans forward a little.

"Two point six million pounds? It's a good value." There's a chuckle through the room, and even the auctioneer smiles. There are no takers at two-six. "Two million five hundred thousand pounds, then, is it?"

Selley holds his gavel for a pregnant moment—it lifts up—and snaps down.

Crack.

"Two million five hundred thousand," Selley announces as the room breaks into applause. "Congratulations. A great acquisition, sir."

Journalists immediately surround the young man; flustered, he shakes his head at any comment and flees. With the auction house's 12 percent fee added in, and converting to dollars, he's just spent $5.8 million in under sixty seconds. It is the most anyone has ever spent for a published work at Sotheby's. The signed copies of Joyce, Wilde, Woolf, and the handwritten papers from Sylvia Plath, Coleridge,

T. E. Lawrence, Charles Dickens—all 506 other lots on sale today—
none even approach the First Folio's price. In fact, all the other lots
combined are still worth millions less than the Folio. The thing is now
worth its weight in gold. Come to think of it—I pause to find an ex-
change rate of $651/oz in the *Guardian* tucked under my arm, and I
biro out the math in a margin—ah, I see that I have misstated its
value, and that it is quite wrong to say that it is worth its weight in
gold.

The Folio is now worth *fifty-five times* its weight in gold.

And that's a very odd thing, because once it was scarcely even
worth its weight in paper.

Half of the crowd instantly pours out of the auction room lugging
camera tripods and tapping at their BlackBerrys, not even waiting
for the next auction lot; the blue-aproned assistant gingerly returns
William to his glass case, opened once again to his watchful title-
page portrait. The poor woman looks rather terrified at handling the
book; today may have been her first time.

She'll remember it for the rest of her days; everyone does. For me,
the first Folio I ever laid hands upon was not a fine calfbound copy
with untrimmed pages like this one. Mine was chopped to pieces
and hiding among some scraggly bushes about a hundred yards behind an Orange Julius stand. I first viewed a Folio at the Sutro Library, a San Francisco archive in an unlovely concrete box just
behind the Stonestown Galleria mall; even scholars scarcely know of
the place. I'd once worked in the mall's candy shop as a student,
swiping sweets in the stockroom while reading Shakespeare on my
breaks, never knowing that I was close enough to hit the real thing
with a well-thrown caramel cream. I couldn't have known—the library is nothing to look at inside or out—a place so underfunded

that, in place of the V-shaped, padded bookholders de rigueur in any rare-book room, they use cardboard wedges that an enterprising staffer has duct-taped together from hacked-up shipping boxes and then covered with tablecloth fabric.

And yet: they have a Folio.

Amid Sutro's sheet-metal cabinets and Formica tabletops is the dusty marble bust of founder Adolph Sutro, a spectacularly mutton-chopped Victorian mining baron. He's forever parted from his much grander library of a century ago: two hundred thousand of Sutro's volumes were incinerated in San Francisco's 1906 earthquake. But the Folio survived, a stroke of luck so remarkable that it made head-line news in the *Times*. You'd hardly guess today that the book bore any relation to this volume in Sotheby's; the Sutro copy is not one volume but twelve, the original pages having been separated into slim volumes of three plays apiece. The first volume's endpapers have grease stains that are suspiciously round and fingerlike; the volumes have messy tears, fault lines that run through the fiber of the text; other volumes have pages flecked with tiny burn holes of a pattern familiar to pipe smokers. In that first volume a Vonnegutian pencil doodle hovers over *Measure for Measure*; turn to *A Midsommer Nights Dreame* and you'll find this penned into the margins:

y y y y y
your your
y
y y y y y y y y y y y y y y y y y y y
your your your your

The hand is recognizable as that taught in the mid-seventeenth century; so, I would guess, is the indescribable scribbling in *King*

John. The first time I held that Folio, my hands quivering like the Sotheby's assistant, I couldn't decide whether to be horrified or delighted by the sacrilege I'd found: some Jacobean brat had been practicing his penmanship exercises on a Shakespeare Folio.

The more Folios you hold, the more of these scribblings you find. The Dr. Williams Folio may be one of the finest in the world, but it still has that ancient vandal in the margins of *Hamlet* inviting readers to kiss his ass. Like the Sutro Folio scribbling, this also appears to date from the mid-1600s; and that coincidence, it turns out, is no juvenile accident at all.

The next lot brought to the Sotheby's lectern looks bewilderingly like the previous lot: the same face, the same type, the same titles, the same pagination.

"Lot ninety-six," Selley announces. "The *Second* Folio of 1632."

The First Folio may seem immortal today, but its creators proved all too perishable. By 1627, just four years after its publication, Jaggard's son Isaac also died. Though local printer Thomas Cotes snapped up the Barbican shop and the Folio rights from Isaac's widow, he couldn't get much help from the original editors. Henry Condell immediately died as well, and just as Cotes had secured permissions from all the play's owners, John Heminge promptly expired in the middle of a local plague outbreak. Shakepeare's players had now vanished; never again would any man be able to speak of Shakepeare's words from the living experience of having walked the boards of the Globe with him.

"£125,000. 130,000?" The bids ricochet around the room. "135,000. 140,000? 145,000 . . ."

Under Cotes's hand the same presses and probably some of the same assistants would now, nine years later, revisit their old work

and reset the entire Folio by hand. They used the First Folio's pagination as a guide and caught nearly seventeen hundred errors from
the first edition. That sounds extraordinary until you realize that's
about two per page, a rate that hardly makes any copy editor drop
their red pencil in shock. *All* books have hundreds or thousands of
errors in manuscript; that's why heaven made copy editors, and why
hell made pedants. But the Second Folio brought another pleasant
find; for this edition, John Milton added a celebratory poem to the
preliminaries. Any sensible customer would have seen the new Folio as at least a small improvement on the old, even if every fix—
changing Macbeth's "weyard" sisters, for instance, into "wayward"
sisters—did not quite find general acceptance.

   "£150,000 . . . £155,000 . . . £160,000 . . ."

   This Second Folio is, if anything, even more used than the First.
The very first page is scribbled from top to bottom in ancient
brown ink. Sworling flourishes crowd over a thistle patch of owners'
names—Will Mille, Alice Monke, John Kent—as well as forgotten
notes to deceased selves. The jottings date to 1661 and 1663, just as a
Third Folio was getting prepared and then released. New editions
nudged old ones onto the used markets and under ill-used pens; after all, new paper was expensive, while page for page an old Folio
was cheap. So why not use it as a scratch pad?

   "£160,000," the gavel cracks down. With the auction house's
premium, that works out to a healthy $343,000.

   The second half of the 1600s was not kind to the Shakespeare
Folios. To the progeny of his original audiences, Shakespeare
seemed dated—so little thought of that thirty-one years passed
between the Second and Third Folios. You could hardly blame the
printers; chunks of the Second Folio languished unassembled in
the old Cotes workshop for nearly a decade after the 1632 run.

Shakespeare had become your grandfather's playwright, less fashion-able even than his old colleague Ben Jonson. By 1652 one published account of major playwrights didn't even include Shakespeare; a publisher, listing a sleek new edition of Beaumont, also noted as an afterthought that it would also eventually "reprint old Shakespeare."

When the Third Folio did finally come out in 1663, Printer's Row was now populated by a generation not yet born when Shakespeare died. One can hardly blame them for stumbling into the oldest of traps: they fell for the fakes. Along with one new and genuine Shakespeare find (*Pericles*), the Third Folio includes a half dozen old mock-Shakespeare chestnuts such as *Locrine*. To a buyer in London's streets, this fattened-up Third Folio must have looked like a great improvement indeed. When Oxford's Bodleian Library received its copy of the new and improved edition, it dutifully got rid of its 1623 Folio. After all, they reasoned, who'd want such an inferior book?

Who indeed?

I slip out between lots, still puzzling over the Folio's purchaser until I spot a Shakespeare scholar in the crowd.

"Who was that buyer on the First Folio?" I hail him. "He looked like he might have bought it for his dorm room."

"Oh, no," he laughs. "He's in someone else's employ."

"Who?" I ask innocently.

"Word's about that it's Simon Finch," the scholar says as we leave the auction rooms. "I'll tell you, Finch's place is right around the corner from here. Let's see if he's in."

We stroll over to Finch's bookshop at 53 Maddox Street, feeling rather clever until we see the small sign in the window:

CLOSED UNTIL JULY 18TH
FOR REDECORATION

"Well," he laughs bitterly. "What do you know."

I peer inside the darkened window. For a place allegedly reopen-
ing in five days, the shop appears curiously abandoned. The only
books visible are a single cardboard box of nineteenth-century volumes with busted spines; the display window has nothing but a
haphazard stack of catalogs—scattered, as if dropped by a surprised
intruder—and next to those, a single, crumpled two-liter bottle of
mineral water. It does not look like the office of a man who just spent
£2.5 million within the last half hour.

"Seems like auspicious timing to lock up your shop and vanish,"
I mutter.

My companion ponders this, then offers the only response one
can give to any mystery in London:

"Let's have some tea," he suggests.

A Folio invites mysteries. The First Folio sold today, for instance,
shouldn't really be there at all. The library left by Dr. Daniel Williams
upon his death in 1716 largely consisted of the book categories you'd
expect from a minister: heavy, theology, and heavy theology. Scattered among his seventy-nine hundred books were an incongruous
handful of plays—including two signed Ben Jonsons—and the un-
fashionable and old volume stamped *Shakespeare* upon its spine. It
owes its survival to its apparent worthlessness. His library bequest
forbade duplicate titles, so that new editions always displaced old
ones. But the theological library and its students were so little interested in Shakespeare that they never bought a replacement volume;
and so, paradoxically, the First Folio's uselessness kept it beautifully
preserved in the Williams collection.

But why own the Folio in the first place? A clue to its presence
lies within a funeral sermon: Dr. Williams is recalled as a man who

"exercis'd a Frugality as to his own Person, possibly to an Excess."
When even friends standing over your freshly dug grave feel moved
to remark upon your cheapness, then it may be surmised that you are
indeed cheap. Like any well-read cheapskate, Williams haunted the
used-book sales, and in 1699 he snagged the estate collection of one
Dr. William Bates, a fellow minister over in Hackney, already famed
as a "devourer of books." It's unlikely that Williams was much interested in the Shakespeare or the Johnson volumes, but the deceased's
house had to be cleared out, and so into the cart they went.

Estate sales were how most Folios changed hands, and the book's
first owner was probably dead back when Bates himself had acquired it. In the endpapers is the notation *John Plomer*, which might
refer to a London cordwainer, or fine shoemaker, known to be active
and prosperous in London in 1623. A will indicates that this same
Plomer may have died in 1649, whereupon the book was probably
sold; the rebinding job on it looks to date to the 1650s. Eventually
Bates bought it, probably while replacing the library he lost in the
Great Fire of 1666, so it may not even have been his *first* First Folio.

The Great Fire had a profound effect on the Folios; it had a
profound effect on all English literature, one that is still little recognized or understood today. If only the names of most plays from
Shakespeare's time survive today, it may be blamed on the nights
of September 2 through 5 of 1666, when a blaze in the bakery
shop of Thomas Farriner turned into a firestorm, then into riots
and wholesale demolitions, and finally into an inferno that en-
gulfed the homes of seventy thousand out of the city's eighty thousand inhabitants.

Initially the city's booksellers were complacent; nobody imagined
that fires a half mile off by London Bridge could possibly reach St.
Paul's. But as the flames marched westward, panicked sellers began

stuffing their stock into the crypts of the cathedral, cramming hundreds of thousands of volumes among the dead bodies. This was virtually the entire stock of literature for sale in the country. The catacombs, bookmen reasoned, had withstood the centuries for a reason; they were a veritable fireproof safe.

As the first embers alighted upon a crude wooden repair patch in the cathedral's roof around eight in the evening, they had reason to think better of this plan.

The roof slowly gathered flame, then rapidly, then with such astonishing speed and heat that pyrogenic lightning—the kind normally generated by forest fires—began flashing over the doomed cathedral. Within an hour the grandest structure in London went up with a roar of crashing beams and shattering glass, and with a burning glare so powerful that one bookseller consoled himself by reading a single volume of poetry that he had saved from his doomed stock. The cathedral fire was so bright in the nighttime, he mused, "as to enable me to read very clearly a 16mo. edition of Terence, which I carried in my pocket."

That's when chunks of the cathedral exploded outward into the square, and the booksellers went running.

"The stones of St. Paul's flew like grenades," recalled one witness, "the melting lead running down the streets in a stream, and very pavements glowing with a fiery redness, so as no horse or man was able to tread on them."

The fire burned itself out the next day, having traversed the city from Pudding Lane before halting at Pie Corner—God will have his little jokes—and in the ruins of St. Paul's and the surrounding precincts, English literature was now written only in ash. The booksellers found ruin in the St. Paul's vaults, and the trade's losses were absolutely staggering in modern terms. Evelyn pegged it at about £200,000 worth at the time, or roughly $160 million today. The country's publishers and booksellers were almost entirely wiped out—as were their customers. A great many First Folios likely resided within the city walls, perhaps scores or even hundreds, before being abandoned to the relentless flames as London readers fled for their lives. The newly printed Third Folio fared worst of all; innumerable unsold copies went up in the flames, ironically making the Third a rarer Folio today than even the First. And the next Sunday, when diarist Samuel Pepys attended a service in one of London's few remaining chapels, he listened as the church's dean addressed a makeshift congregation of miserable and shaken fire-refugees.

"The city," the minister announced, *"is reduced from a large folio to a decimo-tertio."*

So the word is that the Folio's headed abroad.

"They have thirty days to pay for it," Peter Selley explains when I ring him up afterward at Sotheby's. "And they'll need a license."

A license for a book? That can only mean one thing.

"An *export* license?" I nudge.

"Y-eees . . . You need to get an export license for these things. Something that's entirely unique is more likely to be stopped. For instance, some of Lewis Carroll's painted-glass slides. With a Folio, where there's more than one about, that's less likely to be an issue."

The Folio might be the most valuable printed book ever sold in Britain, but it's not unique—so, off it goes to parts unknown. And there was, Selley admits, an extraordinary amount of interest from abroad this time. But then, Folios have always had a certain wanderlust. Not all Folios were left to await the Great Fire's flames, after all. In the 1620s, the Folio made its way across Britain—besides the one to Bodysgallen Hall in Wales, another Folio seems to have made its way to a mathematics professor in Aberdeen—and it may have crossed the sea. The Spanish diplomat Count Gondamar, known to have frequented the Globe in its glory days, is said to have taken one back to Spain. Yet another Folio departed for Padua, the setting for Shakespeare's *Taming of the Shrew*. In fact, he got the geography of Padua wrong in the play; and so Shakespeare's book quickly became better traveled than the man himself ever was.

"So was it an institution?" I badger. "A private buyer?"

"It was for a private collection."

My eyebrows go up at this. Aside from Bond villains, there aren't that many private buyers these days for a five-million-dollar Folio. It's an improbable distance from the first recorded auction sale of a First Folio in 1687, when it sold for just over eight shillings—not even half its original cover price. A fourth and final Folio had just come out a couple of years earlier, printed on extrawide and thick Royal Paper, which rendered all the previous editions just a little shabby. The First Folio became just another raffish, faintly disreputable, old used book.

"I don't suppose . . ." I tap my pencil slowly against my desk. "I don't suppose you can tell me who it was bought for?"

"Ahh," Peter gives a thoughtful pause. "That, I'm afraid, is something I cannot disclose."

"Of course, of course."

Word will get out, someday.

It always does. Maybe not until the new owner dies or goes bankrupt, but it will happen. An executor does not stumble upon a Folio without crying out for everyone to hear. You can track each copy of a Folio over the centuries through these cries of discovery, and from the cries of loss. Folios have been found in Lincolnshire granaries and in Tokyo vaults; they have been lost to fire and torn to pieces and sunk to the bottom of the Arctic Ocean; they have turned up in abandoned Spanish halls and in spinsters' bungalows. The story of each Folio, of each survivor across four centuries from that Barbican print shop, is the story of the vicissitudes of every book after it leaves the author's hands: they are scorned and loved, remade and destroyed, and eternally lost and found again.

And above all else, they are to be found in London.

ACT II

Hampstead Heath, London

DAWN.

At the top of East Heath Road, the Queen Mary nursing home is waking up and turning on its lights; the shafts of light from its windows illuminate the space where the home of George Steevens once stood. You hardly need reminders of mortality at a nursing home, but this plot of land is peculiarly haunted. It was once the home of London's greatest Shakespeare scholar; before then it was the Upper Flask Tavern, so named for its fashionable bottles of Hampstead well water; and before that, it was Upper Bowling Green Tavern, for the simple reason of having a fine bowling green. In every incarnation, it was a home to London's poets and scholars. Swift and Pope drank here under the old mulberry tree; so did Addison and Steele. Samuel Richardson was a regular patron and amused himself by having his heroine Clarissa hide out in the tavern. Only a brick boundary wall is left of the scenery preserved in old engravings; turn the corner to where the mulberry tree and the bowling green once lay, and there's just a clumsy triangle of green and a lichen-stained wooden bench; aged patients sit on it and stare at Vauxhalls lurching by in traffic.

From here, beginning in 1771 and not stopping until 1804, the scholar George Steevens would get up before sunrise and set out upon a daily pilgrimage, crisscrossing London to save the works of William Shakespeare. Follow the path of Steevens, and you follow the path of Shakespeare in eighteenth-century London.

And it's not an easy path to reckon in the daytime, let alone before six A.M.; the buildings are half-gone, the names and numbers changed. Today it's all sturdy Victorians and Edwardians, all steam heat and leaded panes and trimmed shrubs, while between them bursts out the heath's heaping profusions of gnarled and swaying trees. The road quickly disappears down East Heath with a sharp turn into dense woodland and winding footpaths, plunging past Squires Mount and Lady Heath Manor, the sidewalk getting more overgrown until—alarmingly—it stops altogether. I cross the lane onto a dirt and gravel shoulder and wander out into Hampstead Heath. Staggeringly beautiful, messy and unmown; black sparrows swoop down from windy trees, fields of grasses go to seed in the slanted morning rays. Overhead, an airliner disappears steadily into a cloud bank.

A swan fusses its feathers against the water, ruffling them on the surface; the occasional dog snuffles out abandoned badger dens. The Vale feels empty and wild—it always does, and for centuries that's been its greatest feat of urban illusion. It was here that Dickens sent Bill Sikes fleeing after committing murder, though it was really Dickens himself who liked to flee to these fields when he needed somewhere to think. The sights on the heath have not changed too much from Dickens's day, or from Keats's thirty years before him, who lived just over *there*—or from Steevens another thirty years back as he started his daily walk.

Steevens needed the peace and quiet. For when he left his neighborhood and ventured down into the city each day, he entered a decades-long tangle of bibliomania, bitter jealousies, and ruthless competition. And through it all ran a single thread: a battered Folio that Steevens kept in his home by this heath.

A man on the heath is at the head of a great river of urban traffic, and from this tranquil rivulet you pass down into the gathering stream of Hampstead proper. Call it Pramstead: baby carriages weaving, dodging, clattering over pavers—past women in hijabs talking earnestly on a bench, as a young father walks his little boy in circles, semicircles, and occasionally a straight line. I cut past the Free Hospital, where staffers contradictorily smoke out front—down Haverstock, past the Hampstead Hill school sign advertising a PIMM'S AND STRAWBERRIES ON THE LAWN benefit, past the brilliantly named Downside Crescent, and on to the Legal Inn. It sells meeting rooms by the hour in the back and coffee by the cup in the front—so you can pay £2.10 for a cappuccino, or pay £120 for "coffee and initial legal consultation." Were you a publisher sitting here three hundred years ago, the advice would be quite simple: *start buying copyrights.*

When the eighteenth century dawned, a generation had passed since the 1685 Fourth Folio of Shakespeare; and while stalwart old productions like *Macbeth* still trundled along in London theaters, Shakespeare had become a decidedly well-worn literary property. But a careful observer might have known better: he might have known that the entire meaning of literary property was about to change.

Jacob Tonson was that careful observer.

The portly and blunt-spoken scion of an old-school St. Paul's bookseller—his grandfather Matthew had been one of the bookmen wiped out by the Great Fire—Jacob was the greatest wheeler-dealer

British bookselling has ever produced, or perhaps ever will. After setting up shop in 1678, it was Tonson who bothered to buy the rights to a not overly popular work called *Paradise Lost*, and then, in apparent defiance of common sense, he issued it in a sumptuous illustrated edition. It proved to be a brilliant gamble. His eye for acquiring neglected dead geniuses made him rich; his eye for spotting unknown new ones made him influential. By the turn of the century, his drinking cadre, the Kit Kat Club, ruled the summers at the Upper Flask tavern with a heady mix of nobility and writers. And thanks to his profitable grip on London bookselling, if Jacob Tonson wasn't buying you a drink, then you and the books you bought were probably paying for his. He became, to one contemporary, "the Chief merchant to the Muses," and to another, "a pimp or gentleman-usher to the Muses."

Tonson's club, filled as it was with dukes and lords, was quite possibly his most brilliant business venture of all. Not that he would have called it that; but his pleasure had a curious way of serving his business. By the turn of the century, momentum was building for the creation of modern copyright via a piece of legislation known as the Statute of Anne, or the Copyright Act of 1709. In the act, copyright for all new works was granted to the author for a renewable term of fourteen years; but works already in print would be grandfathered in to their *current* owners with a more generous term of twenty-one years. And the new law actually had teeth: unauthorized editions could be pulped and the printers fined a penny per sheet. For those in the know—those, say, at the Kit Kat Club—this produced a handy bit of insider knowledge. Neglected old works, bought cheaply in a market that still gave little value to book rights, could be monopolized under the new, stronger law for decades by quietly buying them up and publishing them before the act was passed.

Jacob set his right-hand man and namesake nephew, Jacob Jr., to work at snapping up literary properties. Junior had particular luck with the heirs of deceased publishers; the inadvertent owners of hundreds of near-derelict works, they were happy to unload the stuff cheaply. From one estate he acquired some two hundred copyrights for £140, and from another he gained roughly three hundred more copyrights for £100—in all, over five hundred copyrights for £240, or an average price of about ten shillings apiece. Much of it was hopeless stuff, literary sweepings from the floor of the printer's shop—but along with the rubbish, Jacob Jr. had acquired all of John Dryden, all of John Donne, and the complete works of Beaumont and Fletcher. And, it so happened, among those ten-shilling purchases there was also this entry: *Mr William Shakespears Plays.*

Double-deckers on the Old Kent line roar by outside; an early-morning jogger stops out front at a red drop box to send off his gas bill, then bustles off past the Sir Richard Steele Tavern. Along with Steele—who owned this very plot of land—a bevy of other writers less known to us today used to make their way up this stretch of Haverstock to the Kit Kat meetings. One of the best known to Londoners in 1708 was Nicholas Rowe; a rather slovenly fellow a little too fond of slouching down at the Cocoa Tree inn and borrowing snuff from his friends, Rowe was nonetheless a highly enough esteemed talent that he eventually became poet laureate. But in 1708, Rowe was on a losing streak. He'd just had three poorly received plays in a row, which may have made him that loveliest of all creatures to a commissioning editor: the Celebrated Author Who Needs Money.

Perhaps, the Kit Kat host suggested, he'd like to edit an edition of Shakespeare?

Rowe most certainly did.

The elder Jacob wasn't interested in churning out another Shakespeare folio: that wasn't his publishing house's style. A savvy traveler with an eye on the superior work of continental printers, Tonson had helped lead the trend away from London's decidedly old-fashioned tendency toward massive folios by producing handsome and aggressively protected octavo editions of English authors. He knew his readers wanted the stylish, small books that they'd seen Dutch travelers reading—easy to fit into a coat pocket, easy to carry to a pleasant garden bench—the sort of volume that instead of needing special furniture to support it, you could simply hold open in the palm of your hand. Chop out anything that looked old-fashioned, Tonson realized, and add in striking engravings, biographies, and forewords by famous contemporary authors, and you had yourself a whole new market, even for books that people already owned the fusty old editions of.

And so he set Rowe to work. First came the matter of the physical direction of the plays: they were a mess. Entrances and exits were unmarked in the folios, as indeed were many act and scene divisions. Rowe, as one of London's greatest playwrights of the era, was perfectly suited for the task: he added a complete set of the now-familiar act and scene divisions, as well as the stage directions largely missing from the Folios. For the first time, readers who weren't playwrights themselves could readily comprehend Shakespeare as a literary reading experience in its own right.

As it happened, one of Rowe's theatrical friends—the elderly actor Thomas Betterton—was planning a pilgrimage to Stratford to capture the last remaining memories of Shakespeare among the locals. While nobody still alive had known Shakespeare, their parents and grandparents had. The oral history Betterton found about

the playwright's genealogy and his early days as a schoolmaster, a
deer poacher, and a local wag—in short, most of the colorful stories
we know about the man—survive solely because of the old actor's
journey and Rowe's decision to use them in his preface.

Amid these investigations, Rowe and Tonson also made a be-
lated effort to find old copies of Shakespeare's work. Readers of
the *Daily Courant* on March 19, 1709, found this last-minute announcement:

> Whereas very Neat and Correct edition of Mr Wm Shake-
> spear's Works in 6 Volumes in Octavo, Adorn'd with Cutts,
> is no so near finish'd as to be publish'd in a Month . . . If
> therefore any Gentleman who have materials by them that
> may be Serviceable to this design will be pleas'd to transmit
> the same to Jacob Tonson at Gray's-Inn-Gate, it will par-
> ticular Advantage to the work, and acknowledg'd as a favour
> by the gentleman who had hath care of this Edition.

If that reads more like an advertisement for a book already close to
completion, there's a reason that their casting call for old editions
was so perfunctory: for legal purposes, Tonson had Rowe base his
text on the Fourth Folio copyrights that he'd purchased. Yet Rowe
did make a few useful discoveries among some scattered quartos:
comparing the Fourth Folio with an old *Hamlet*, Rowe found an entire scene with Fortinbras missing. Another comparison netted the
prologue to *Romeo and Juliet*.

When the collected works came off the presses a month later, the
First Folio's apparent absence in the book's creation seems not to
have bothered anyone, least of all Rowe himself: "I have taken some
Care to redeem him from the Injuries of former Impressions," he

notes proudly. The message to readers was clear: if you had a First Folio, you might as well get rid of it now.

And that's just what many of them did.

A walk from the old meeting place of the Kit Kat down toward Tonson's offices—the same daily pilgrimage Steevens later made—drills you down through a core sample of London. Haverstock retains its Georgian homes and wide sidewalks, but with just a slight change in angle toward Camden—announced with the first boarded-up building in miles—the street changes, as if that angle bottles up all that is Belsize and all that is Camden to either side of it. Here were Georgians and heath; now come council flats, sooty Victorians, boarded-up shops, and abandoned wrappers. Chalk Farm Road appears; so do chip shops, the Salvation Army, and slogan T-shirts. Trees and hedges disappear. Past the frontage of Chalk Farm Tires—altogether surreal if misread—the boutiques change to stalls, an endless thud-thud-thud of house music; stands of army boots, cheap scarves, and bumping crowds funneling down past Camden Lock, where I stand on an arching bridge and watch two women hop off a barge and struggle fetchingly with the lock levers. The crowds thicken at Tottenham and solidify by Oxford Street, with everyone rushing to work. Two hours in and you are as far as possible from the wild empty fields of Hampstead Heath.

Gray's Inn comes as a relief: a long, tree-lined promenade encircled by old brick law offices, all enclosed by gates and porters; through its archway, bustling London fades as you walk to the center of the immense quadrangle. In Tonson's time, the barristers here also made their homes in these buildings; their children rolled hoops and whooped through these fashionable precincts, darting among gardens originally laid out by Sir Francis Bacon. At this end of Gray's

Inn, Jacob Tonson's shop gave the place its quorum of slightly ragged students and scholars; Tonson would rent new books out by the day, to be read in the store, making his shop as busy and learned as any library.

The new edition of Shakespeare by Rowe sold well, though at thirty shillings for a set, Tonson clearly had no interest in the masses. Like holders of monopolies ever since, he was shoring up profits against the high-volume, low-margin sales to follow after the copyright ran out; for now, with exclusive control over Shakespeare's work, the trick was to focus on the wealthy few who could pay a high markup. And those customers seemed pleased enough with the new edition; it was far more readable than the folios of old, and no one was much troubled about the Fourth Folio being the source of the text—that was the last edition, and therefore surely the best.

Even as he was arranging the reprinting of Shakespeare, the elder Tonson was still keeping an eye on future talents as well; in his Gray's Inn shop he penned this letter to a promising eighteen-year-old poet:

> Sir,—I have lately seen a pastoral of yours in mr Walsh's and mr Congreve's hands, which is extreamly ffine & is generally approv'd off by the best Judges in poetry. I Remember I have formerly seen you at my shop & am sorry I did not Improve my Acquaintance with you. If you design your Poem for the Press no person shall be more Carefull in the printing of it, nor no one can give a greater Incouragement; than Sir Your Most Obedient
>
> > Humble Servant
> > Jacob Tonson.
>
> > *Pray give me a line. Per post.*

The letter was addressed to a young "Mr. Pope" in the village of Binfield. It was to be the beginning of Alexander Pope's decades-long reign as London's leading wit and critic, an association that was fortunate indeed for the Tonsons. Renewing the Shakespeare copyright meant that every fourteen years they had to produce a new edition; but when it came time to start planning for a 1723 edition, their faithful Mr. Rowe was long dead. In the meantime, Pope's *Rape of the Lock* had secured his place as the era's leading poet, his *Essay on Criticism* had made him a titan of contemporary writing about literature, and his translations of the *Iliad* and the *Odyssey* had made him the era's most powerful editor. The choice for Shakespeare's new champion was clear.

Pope was not an easy man to work with: he had the great gift of being a literary genius, and the great impediment of reminding others of that fact. And although Tonson's edition was rushed into print by the 1723 legal deadline—the printing so hurried that some pages were clapped together with the ink still wet—their resident genius was maddeningly slow in finishing his preface for it. The all-but-finished volumes, still unbound, simply sat in the publisher's offices. As late as December 1724, the correspondence between the two finds Tonson still pleading with his poet for the preface: "I beg to have it, for I am impatient to publish." Without the inimitable voice of Pope in a personal introduction, Tonson knew his volume lacked its greatest selling point. The books simply had to wait for the poet to stir himself into action.

When it was released at long last in 1725, Pope's new edition looked strikingly different from any Shakespeare before. Priced at a stiff six pounds, it was even more clearly aimed at the wealthy. But when the first copies went on sale, it wasn't here by the stately promenade of Gray's Inn. The Tonsons had moved to the considerably more aggressive hustle of the streets down by the river and, to mark the change, had a new portrait painted on the store's hanging sign.

Customers looking for Jacob Tonson now simply followed the directions printed on the title page of his books:

at Shakespeare's Head
over-against Catherine-street in the Strand

Walk down to the corner today, and there's no trace left of the considerable reputation it had back in Tonson's day. Not for books, mind you; for prostitution and for theater. "Oh, may thy virtue guard thee through roads / Of Drury's mazy courts and dark abodes! / The harlot's guileful paths, who nightly stand, / Where Catherine Street descends into the Strand," one poet was moved to write not long after Tonson's move there. It would remain such on Steevens's walks decades later, and indeed long after: the better part of two centuries after the move, another writer excoriated this corner for its "trade in flesh and blood ... Catherine Street were gay indeed, if wine and prolificacy in the lowest and worst reality of its forms are ever gay." Enough Londoners certainly seemed to think it was, and so for many years Shakespeare's portrait kept watch over bards by day, and over bawds by night.

If the two great industries of Catherine Street were walking the boards and walking the streets, it's hard to say which Alexander Pope considered less reputable. His preface, finally delivered to Tonson, revealed that he'd gathered old copies of Shakespeare's plays—twenty-seven of them, in fact, making his perhaps the first Shakespeare library ever assembled. Newspaper notices as early as 1721 had sought out old quartos to compare in the hope of creating a definitive edition of Shakespeare. But in his preface, Pope revealed that he considered the Folio a perversion of the more honest Shakespeare to be found in these early quartos.

The First Folio was, he declared, "in all respects . . . far worse than the Quartos. First, because of the addition of trifling and bombast[ic] passage are in this edition far more numerous . . . [while] a number of beautiful passages which are extant in the first editions are omitted." When not puffing up the plays with poorly written ad-libs for themselves and their friends, he insinuated, Heminge and Condell were mutilating them by chopping out any passages that challenged their lazy temperaments. Far from saving Shakespeare, Pope charged, the "Impertinence of his first Editors" had committed assault and battery upon him.

His evidence for Heminge and Condell's literary crimes was rather peculiar: like obscenity, Pope knew adulterated Shakespeare when he saw it. And he saw it in "a great number of mean conceits and ribaldries . . . the low scenes of Mobs, Plebeians and Clowns." Comedies, it seems, were especially prone in Pope's eyes to not really being Shakespeare. Even if the former deer stealer, glovemaker's son, and longtime actor had been no more elevated in background than his fellow players, Pope nonetheless refused to believe that a man capable of writing Hamlet's soliloquy could also have stooped to lowbrow entertainments.

Pope's readers found that he had therefore obligingly cut some fifteen hundred lines out of Shakespeare's plays, banishing them to the footnotes—or, as he put, "degraded to the bottom of the page"— with such comments as "trash" (*Othello*), "nonsense" (*Romeo and Juliet*), and "the lowest and most trifling conceits, to be accounted for only from the gross taste of the age he liv'd in" (*Two Gentlemen of*

Verona). And so Britain's greatest living poet had, with the swift rapier thrusts of his quill, defended the honor of London's greatest dead poet from the vicious depredations of the First Folio. It should have been one of the crowning glories of Alexander Pope's career.

That's not how it turned out.

Catherine Street, London

STEEVENS WAS A broad-shouldered, striding sort; he had to be, walking every day through a fifteen-mile circuit of mud and horse-shit between Hampstead and the Thames. To do this for thirty years, you must have a great love—or at least a great tolerance—for your fellow city-dwellers. You become exquisitely attuned to urban topography, to the subtle gradients of zoning, of building styles, of people. And walking down the Strand today, past the Inns of Court and up Chancery Lane, what you begin to sense is increasing wealth: this is a street of bank vaults and brass-plate accountancies, leading inevitably to the legal Valhalla of Lincoln's Inn Fields, the largest open space in the old City precincts. For Steevens, there would also have been a sense of history: here, during the inn's construction, a young Ben Jonson got an unlikely break. A nobleman passing by overheard a teen laborer speaking of Homer—not the sort of thing you generally hear at a construction site then or now. After some earnest conversation between the two, the teenaged Ben Jonson was a bricklayer for his father-in-law no more: he had his first noble patron.

Lincoln's Inn was, like so many London streets, much rougher in the old days. The poet John Gay—he who warned of the Catherine

Street harlots—had little comfort to give walkers along the outer wall of Lincoln's Inn. It was populated at night with sham cripples waiting to pounce upon the unwary: "That crutch, which late compassion moved, shall wound / Thy bleeding head, and fell thee to the ground." That wasn't the only devilry to be found in these precincts at night: there was also the New Theatre. Built by impresario John Rich in 1714, it did a roaring trade in second-class theater known as pantomime. Think of it as Cirque du Soleil in powdered wigs: they used little dialogue but a maximum of heavy-handed music, dazzling acrobatics, flashy costumes, and stage effects, all gussied up with vaguely high-minded mythological and historical themes. The loathing the literati felt for these productions was only matched by their immense popularity. And sitting in the midst of it all, slapping together such ludicrous moneymakers as *Merlin: The Devil of Stonehenge*, was Lewis Theobald.

Theobald was born just a month before Pope in 1688 and, like Pope, was a prodigy; despite apprenticing as a lawyer, by the age of twenty-one he was debuting his play *The Persian Princess* on Drury Lane. Pope's literary debut followed just months later. And like Pope, Theobald worked for London bookseller Bernard Lintot as a reliable hand at translation, tackling volumes of Plato and Aeschylus; early in their careers, their translations of separate parts of Ovid's *Metamorphoses* were combined and sold as "by Mr. Pope and Mr. Theobald." Pope, however, had the famed wit and the meteoric rise; Theobald was a plodder and fell back sheepishly on pantomime scripts to support himself. But he still watched his peer from afar in admiration, and in a 1721 collection unveiled his homage "To Mr. Pope on His Translation of Homer." Theobald declared that Pope's skill would make later ages think English was the epic bard's original language: "So much, Pope, thy English Iliad charms / When pity melts us, or other passion warms, That after ages shall with wonder seek / Who 'twas translated *Homer* into *Greek*." Pope was moved to buy four copies of the book.

Soon it was Theobald's turn to buy a book of Pope's. "It was no small Satisfaction therefore to me," he wrote, "when I first heard Mr. POPE had taken upon him the Publication of SHAKESPEARE." If Pope or Tonson were waiting to hear a further hearty congratulations, though, they had a surprise waiting for them. On April 5, 1726—scarcely a year after Pope's release, and with hundreds of copies of the Pope edition still sitting on Tonson's shelves over at Catherine Street—the publisher and author were instead greeted by this slender volume coming across their desks:

Shakespeare Restored

Or, A Specimen of the Many Errors, As Well Committed,
as Unamended, by Mr. POPE
In his Late Edition of this Poet. Designed Not only to correct
the said Edition, but to restore the True Reading of
Shakespeare in all the Editions ever yet publish'd.
by Mr. THEOBALD

In an instant, their years of work were about to implode.

Shakespeare Restored was, quite simply, like nothing any critic in London had ever seen before.

Lewis Theobald held great esteem for Pope; but he had an even higher esteem for Shakespeare, whose work he adapted for the theater, and whose poetry he'd even imitated in his own early volumes. As a classical scholar accustomed to carefully comparing corrupt copies to try to divine a missing original text, he was keenly aware of just how badly preserved Shakespeare's work had become in just a single century. "Thro' the *Indolence*, what thro' the *Ignorance* of his EDITORS," his volume begins, "we have scarce any Book in the *English* Tongue more fertile of Errors . . . [a] vast Crop of Errors, which has almost choak'd up his *Beauties*."

"And I am very sorry," he added, "there is still reason to complain."

Reading Pope's edition—expensive, long-delayed, presumed to be the best yet—must have been one of the great literary disappointments of Theobald's life. Instead of reviving Shakespeare, Pope had buried him under his own carelessness and self-regard—penning a hasty introduction, removing lines he didn't like, and consulting the original texts in such a slipshod fashion that on virtually every page Theobald *knew* Pope was wrong. And yet, here he was—a hack—a pantomime writer—an underpaid translator. Theobald sat in his chambers, surrounded by a vast personal library of old English and classical works that *he* actually bothered to consult, and pondered what to do.

Then—slowly, methodically—he demolished London's greatest poet.

Shakespeare Restored could have been titled *Hamlet Restored*; 132 of its 194 pages are devoted to a page-by-page, line-by-line correction of every single mistake by Pope in that most emblematic of Shakespeare's plays. Some of the mistakes were minor omissions, as in the first scene, when Marcellus beholds the ghost: *Shall I strike it with my partizan?* "The Versification manifestly halts here without any Necessity," Theobald admonishes. "The second Edition in Folio, printed in 1632, and which one of those that Mr. POPE professes to have collated, makes out the Numbers of this line by reading: *Shall I strike AT it with my partizan?*"

Even if Pope had assembled a library of old Shakespeare texts,

Theobald implied, he'd been unforgivably sloppy in actually using them. In fact, Pope hardly seemed to have read *any* Shakespeare edition with sufficient care. After noting Pope's rejection of a noun turned into a verb—"to business with the King"—Theobald produces examples from other Shakespeare plays of the bard's fondness for coining new verbs from nouns. We might not think of *paragon* as a verb, but it turns up thus in *Othello*: "That *paragons* Description and wild Fame." Theobald effortlessly produces examples from another seventeen Shakespeare plays before finally halting himself offhandedly, with the blasé remark "I am afraid I am growing too luxuriant in Examples." And then, just to twist the knife, he gives six more.

Ah, but he was just being helpful. Theobald cannily produced the volume in a matching size and binding so that it could be sold as a companion volume to the Pope; unamused purchasers of the six-pound edition could lay the books side by side and ink in all the corrections. "I have so great an esteem for Mr. POPE," Theobald claimed, "and so high an Opinion of his Genius and Excellencies, that I beg to be excused from the least Intention of derogating from his Merits." But Theobald's choice of *Hamlet* for *Shakespeare Restored* could not have been more derogatory. If he could find 132 pages of errors by Pope in Shakespeare's most scrutinized play, he hinted, then surely there could be *thousands* of pages of corrections for the complete works.

And there was more. Theobald hadn't simply found some missing lines in Pope's edition. He also had found an entire missing play.

While the First Folio might have been the greatest literary rescue mission in the English language, it didn't save *every* play of Shakespeare's. In fact, Jaggard's attempts to secure permission for one play—*Troilus and Cressida*—came so perilously close to failing that the first few Folios off his press didn't even have it. Two more plays—*Pericles* and *The Two Noble Kinsmen*—were not formally included in Shakespeare's works for decades more. These were the lucky ones, snatched from the jaws of oblivion; but others went right down its throat. The most infamous case is that of *Love's Labour's Wonne*, a *Love's Labour's Lost* sequel that turns up in bookseller records as early as 1598; many modern editions of *Lost* note its missing sibling. Most obscure of all, in the very furthest corner of the Shakespeare canon, is *The History of Cardenio*. Performed at the Globe in 1613 and attributed in later Stationer's Company records to Beaumont and Fletcher and a near-retired Shakespeare, it was an adaptation from Cervantes— something that showed Shakespeare in 1613 was still in fine fettle at conjuring the latest entertainments, as *Don Quixote* had only just been translated into English months earlier.

Cardenio is the one other known missing Shakespeare play. But to Lewis Theobald, sitting in his apartment off Great Russell Street after the triumph of *Shakespeare Restored*, it wasn't missing at all. In fact, he said he owned three separate manuscripts of it.

"Is has been alleg'd as incredible," he admitted, "that such a Curiosity should have been stifled and lost to the World for above a Century." But *Cardenio* had skirted the edges of the collected *Works* for years. Thomas Betterton—the old actor who had journeyed to Stratford for Rowe's 1709 collection—had, by Theobald's account, come into possession of a *Cardenio* manuscript. Some drama seems to have surrounded the manuscript's discovery; after it was quietly brought to Drury Lane Theatre in 1709 with a view to staging it, an anonymous letter to a local newspaper claimed that a squabble had shelved the unveiling of a valuable manuscript: "I mean a Play written by Beaumont and Fletcher, and the immortal Shakespear, in the Maturity of his Judgement, a few Years before he dy'd."

Several manuscript copies appear to have been in circulation seventeen years later, when Theobald acquired them. But instead of simply publishing *Cardenio*, Theobald did something more savvy: he rewrote it. It's hard to think of a more sacrilegious act today than rewriting a lost Shakespeare manuscript, but it was common enough practice in Theobald's time to heavily adapt the bard. Even as Theobald was acquiring *Cardenio*, Drury Lane was staging a shambolic *Macbeth* that featured pantomime and a children's clog dance. Theobald may have been a purist at preserving Shakespeare, but he had no qualms with adaptations that were labeled as such.

In fact, Theobald was already an old hand at it; he'd heavily reworked *Richard II* for a profitable run a few years earlier, throwing out entire acts when it suited him, and nearly obliterating others with new writing. As a writer who knew how to pack a house, Theobald also knew that Georgian audiences found unvarnished Elizabethan plays to be impossibly old-fashioned; they had nearly as hard a time understanding Shakespeare as we do. In 1710, the bishop of Rochester made a complaint strikingly familiar to every high schooler who's ever suffered through a Shakespeare assignment: "I protest to you, in an hundred places I cannot construe him, I don't understand him. The hardest part of Chaucer is more intelligible . . . There are Allusions in him to a hundred things, of which I knew nothing, & can guess nothing."

The trick, then, was to *fix Cardenio*—tidy up the composition, dab new clothes on the characters and modernize the diction, dapple some pleasant sunshine over the dreary old thing, and rename it *Double Falshood*. To read Theobald's play today is to scrape in vain at gaudy overcoats of paint, hoping to find the old masterpiece

irretrievably hidden underneath. Shakespeare was only one of perhaps three authors of the original play—and now he was further
hidden under a fourth. Still, Theobald was known to leave at least
some original material behind. For all the reworking that he once
performed upon *Richard II*, he did not alter every line of the play.
Looking closely at *Double Falshood* reveals surviving constructions
typical of Fletcher, who presumably either wrote much of the play
or needed the least revising of the three coauthors. But some spots
that *do* sound uncannily like Shakespeare peek through. Take for
instance, this soliloquy by the heartbroken Henriquez:

> *Where were the Eyes, the Voice, the various Charms,*
> *Each beauteous Particle, each nameless Grace,*
> *Parents of glowing love? All these in Her,*
> *It seems, were not: but a Disease in Me,*
> *That fancied Graces in her——.*

If that's not Shakespeare, then it's certainly one of the most skillful
mimicries ever made of his work. And so, too, are passing lines like "I
profess, a Fox might earth in the Hollowness of your Heart"—or in
one silenced character's pithy rebuke of "Sir, if I must speak Nothing,
I will hear Nothing." In these lines one can still see flashes of brilliance from that original manuscript in Theobald's chambers.

Yet Theobald's financial instincts were absolutely correct. *Double
Falshood* had a profitable run on Drury Lane in December 1727, and
he parlayed its popularity into yet more money by selling the copyright for a tidy £105. And here, in Wild Court, just off Lincoln's Inn
Fields—in dingy quarters that have now been gone for over a
century—the publisher John Watts promptly set about printing the
play. He did it without one of his best workers—a clever journeyman

named Ben Franklin, who'd recently departed for America—but on the whole Watts and Theobald alike seem to have done rather well off the entire affair.

All told, Theobald had quite possibly netted more money from this one play than Pope had made for editing all thirty-six Shakespeare plays.

Pope could take it no longer. The criticism of his Shakespeare had been humiliating enough—like getting "knocked on the head with a pisspot" he groused to his friend Jonathan Swift—but to see Theobald swanning around London with his lucrative "new" Shakespeare play was simply too much. To make matters worse, Theobald was now announcing that he'd be creating his own editions of single plays, almost daring Pope and Tonson to come after him.

Pope rose to the bait, taking a swipe at the dogged scholarship of Theobald, "who thinks he reads when he but scans and spells / A Word-catcher, that lives on Syllables." Theobald immediately responded with a public letter that calmly detailed another Pope error—this time in *The Merchant of Venice*—and promised that, if asked, "I'll give him five hundred more fair emendations." The rest of the year would become a Punch-and-Judy show between the two. One month later Pope unleashed his mock-heroic epic *The Dunciad*, centered on a dunce named Tibbald who destroys improvements upon Shakespeare in the dreaded name of accuracy:

> *Here studious I unlucky moderns save,*
> *Nor sleeps one error in its father's grave,*
> *Old puns restore, lost blunders nicely seek,*
> *And crucify poor Shakespeare once a week.*

Theobald's response? Three weeks later he threatened plans for a three-volume set to outline *all* of Pope's errors. The world would get those five hundred errors, and then some. Pope responded by reissuing *The Dunciad* with mock-scholarly footnotes.

London's literati had a good laugh over all this; *The Dunciad* became the very model of poetic satire, fixing Theobald in the popular imagination as a tin-eared killjoy. But one person wasn't laughing. Sitting in his bookstore on Catherine Street, Jacob Tonson Jr. had hundreds of copies of Pope's Shakespeare gathering dust on his shelves. Underneath the witty repartee, Pope had no real answer to Theobald's unyielding cross-examinations. The tainted volumes of Pope became so unsalable that eventually the sets were unloaded for sixteen shillings apiece, a mere eighth of their original price—no more, in fact, than the asking price of a lowly used First Folio.

Theobald Road presents a modern stretch of glass and steel and concrete; when you have a postwar building called Churchill House taking up half the block, it's a good sign that war was involved in the renovation. But before this was Theobald Road, it was simply a road where Theobald *lived*—a section of Great Russell Street where Theobald would trudge into the obscure siding of Wyan's Court, and up to his lodgings. By 1731 Theobald was laboring under terrible infirmities and was deeply in debt; he had only to look at the fate of fellow Wyan's Court resident Elizabeth Thomas—poet and critic, and another target of the *Dunciad*—to wonder whether he, too, might be thrown in debtor's prison for years and then left to die alone in meager lodgings. Pope was living comfortably off a successful translation of the *Odyssey* and was already considered the great immortal wit of the age; Theobald was a dogged scholar with an immense collection of books and an empty wallet. Pope publicly insinuated, in a crowning humiliation, that Theobald was having to pawn his precious scholarly library.

But when the time came to begin editing a new edition of Shakespeare, Pope heard only silence—and Jacob Tonson strolled a few blocks up to Theobald's humble quarters in Wyan's Court.

It was, Pope roared, enough "to make one Spew."

Theobald took up his new editorship with gusto. After quickly putting out a call in newspapers for old copies of Shakespeare, Tonson and Theobald assembled an impressive library of old editions to consult from, including the First and Second Folios; what was more, Theobald's 800-volume personal collection of old English plays and other vernacular literature gave him a pitch-perfect sense of the language of Shakespeare's era. Where Pope had stricken the phrase *more better* in *The Tempest*, Theobald brought it back—because, he pointed out, such double comparatives are both all over the First Folio *and* other books of Shakespeare's time. In a staggering 1,355 notes over seven volumes, Theobald snowed his critics under with evidence from other sixteenth- and seventeenth-century plays, restoring Shakespeare's words by going back to contemporaries and, above all, to the First Folio—an edition that, he suggested wickedly in a footnote, he knew Pope "had not seen."

The call went out in letters and local papers: on January 24, 1734, Theobald's Shakespeare would be ready. It must have been quite a sight. Theobald had a personal subscriber list accounting for five hundred copies, and rather than picking up the book at Tonson's, he'd invited them all to stop by at Wyan's Court that day to pick up their new book. Much of London's aristocracy bought copies, and its far more reasonable price of two pounds—a third of what Pope's edition cost—meant that Theobald's edition also counted London scholars and artists among its buyers. This street saw a procession of such intellectual luminaries as Samuel Richardson, William Hogarth, and Hans Sloane, all coming to pick up the book that it seemed Theobald had been auditioning for all his life. Novelist Henry Fielding, upon examining his copy, hailed Theobald as the man who had saved the national poet from Pope: "Shakespeare by him restor'd again we see / Recover'd of the wounds he bore from thee."

Theobald threw one last haymaker to make sure that Pope never staggered back to his feet again. In an appendix in the final volume, Theobald listed a hierarchy of sources. This was a new notion altogether, and by his reckoning there were ultimately only two collected "Editions of Authority": the First Folio of 1623, and the Second Folio of 1632. The two Folios, once treated as mere old tat, now took on a different light: these were to become respected as the only two printed within any living memory of Shakespeare. The Third and Fourth Folios he deemed to be of "Middle Authority"—and crushingly, Rowe and Pope came under the heading "Editions of no Authority."

And with that, Pope and Theobald's argument was over.

The new edition and editor were both a smashing success. But just as Jacob Tonson was putting out one fire, another was bursting into flame. Within weeks, rival printer Robert Walker issued an impudent announcement promising fourpenny editions of each of Shakespeare's plays. Tonson's monopoly over Shakespeare for three decades, which he'd used to cream off his market with overpriced high-end editions, was suddenly under attack by penny-grubbers. Worse still, deep down he knew he hadn't any legitimate defense at all against it.

Although he could keep a lock on updated modern editions by pumping out a new one every decade, Tonson's copyright over the original old Folio and quartos—the monopoly he'd landed with his lobbying back in 1709—had actually quietly lapsed as of April 10, 1731. At first, Tonson was able to browbeat any other printers eyeing Shakespeare. But Walker was different. Holed up in Turn-Again Lane—a dead-end street from the Old Bailey courthouse, and thus a proverbial spot for dissipation—Walker was a hard-headed character who relished printing political-opposition pamphlets and sensational memoirs. He pioneered the cultivation of the poorest readers by issuing books in four one-penny weekly installments— only a third of what Tonson charged for his cheapest one-shilling copies.

Just to rub it in, Walker had also put a new sign up over his shop—Shakespeare's head. That was *Tonson's* sign. Walker could not have been more provoking if he'd flown the Jolly Roger from his rooftop.

Tonson's attorney sent letters threatening a lawsuit over the Shakespeare reprints, and promising jail for Walker and ruin for his family. Tonson, he said, would spend a thousand pounds—*a thousand pounds!*—preparing his case against Walker. A bookseller who lives on a street full of boozing attorneys is not likely to be impressed by such letters. The maneuver was purely intended to intimidate, and when Walker marched over to Tonson's shop and demanded to see the old man, he admitted that the family didn't have any right to the plays. Where threats would not work, Tonson tried bribery: would the good Mr. Walker take £200 a year to leave Shakespeare alone? The good Mr. Walker would not—and furthermore, his shop assistants wouldn't either, because soon Tonson found himself attacked in the Old Bailey by claims that he'd tried offering them a guinea apiece to sabotage Walker's press. To remind everyone of the hash that Tonson and Pope had once made of Shakespeare, Walker made a public announcement pointing out errors in Tonson's shilling editions of the plays, charging that they were "useless and unintelligible . . . a *Gallimaufry* of Scraps and Nonsense."

Over the next year, Walker issued all of Shakespeare's plays, and what had been a hushed legal struggle became a running battle in London bookstalls. If he couldn't scare or buy Walker off, Tonson decided, he'd bury him. Whenever Walker announced a new play to be published for four pennies, Tonson struck back with a three-penny edition, massive print runs, and ads claiming that it was Walker who had "useless, pirated, and maimed Editions." Tonson was losing money, but he didn't care; Walker was far more than a danger to his Shakespeare monopoly. The Tonsons had hundreds of other old copyrights that had also expired, and preventing their loss meant making an example of this upstart. But Walker had his own tricks: experienced at using a distribution network of agents in other cities to market everything from books to patent medicines, he deftly circumvented Tonson's London-based sales, even promising free delivery—a virtually unheard-of notion in those days. The artist William Hogarth was so amused by the whole affair that he issued a satirical print of Tonson and Walker brawling, titled *The Rival Printers.*

When the smoke had cleared in the late summer of 1735, the literary landscape of Britain was permanently changed. Tonson, in his desperation to crush Walker, may have issued as many as ten thousand copies of *each* Shakespeare play—a shocking figure for that time, leaving the country awash in hundreds of thousands of cheap copies. Shakespeare's plays, though much loved, had never warranted anything remotely close to these print runs. They just happened to be the bullets in the publishing shoot out of the century.

• • •

It's only a short walk from Turn-Again to St. Paul's Churchyard, one that takes you from the legal precincts of the Old Bailey and into what was once the thriving printers' quarters of Paternoster Row and spills you out into the churchyard. Today the churchyard is a place of perhaps misplaced reverence for quiet, but a few centuries ago, this churchyard was regaining the lively bustle that it had so catastrophically lost in the Great Fire. The bookstalls along here would have been a fine place to buy a new Tonson threepenny edition, or a shabby, old Jaggard Folio.

The 1730s are the absolute low point of Folio history; despite Theobald's praise hidden in his appendices and footnotes, Heminge and Condell's edition was worth little in a market swollen with cheap and handsome new editions. It's possible that more Folios were discarded during this era than any other time short of the Great Fire of 1666. And yet something changed in 1734 and 1735. Theobald's zeal in proving Pope wrong had almost single-handedly created a tradition of painstakingly exact Shakespeare scholarship and indeed created the very idea that a sometimes profane and popular native playwright *could* be argued over as intensely as any Greek or Roman classic. And thanks to a bitter price war, Tonson and Walker had inadvertently made Shakespeare available to everyone with a few pennies in their pocket. Without anyone much noticing, the paradoxical foundations of Shakespeare's canonization—that he was the artist of the masses and of scholars alike—had now been laid.

None of those involved would realize just what they had done. Both Tonson Sr. and Tonson Jr. passed away within months of their battle with Walker; they left a gargantuan combined estate of £140,000, showing just how fearsomely deep-pocketed of an opponent Walker had taken on. Nor would Pope or Theobald ever take up their battles again. Just as both had been born months apart, they died months apart in 1744. Pope passed peacefully in his comfortable villa in Twickenham with his friends in attendance; Theobald, ailing and impoverished, died forgotten in his rooms on Wyan's Court. He had just one mourner at his funeral—a faithful stage-prompter who had worked alongside him for years at the Lincoln's Inn Fields theater. But a month later, a surprise awaited Londoners, not least those who'd believed Pope's cruel joke that Theobald had pawned his library.

Lewis Theobald had left behind his books—*lots* of books.

Six hundred and thirty-one lots, to be exact. It took four nights of auctioning in this corner of the St. Paul's Churchyard to dispose of all rare lots from Theobald's shelves. The St. Paul's Coffee-House was the host; normally it was the smoky haunt of writers, printers, and—above all—underemployed parsons who, rather like theological day laborers, sat around in scruffy clerical garb waiting for pickup sermon and burial jobs. But the long, rather plain room also had a sideline in hosting bookish estate auctions: it was known in the first half of the 1700s as the place to go whenever a local bibliomaniac keeled over.

The auction's *Catalogue of the Library of Lewis Theobald, esq., Deceas'd* reveals a treasure trove of literary finds, with everything from an original folio of Ben Jonson's *Works* and a "very ancient" Chaucer folio to—of all things—a new edition of *The Dunciad*. Pope's Shakespeare also turns up, "with many thousand Remarks, some curious, some shrewd, wrote in every Page, by Mr. Theobald." Then there's the mysterious Lot 460: "One hundred ninety-five old English Plays in Quarto, some of them so scarce as not to be had at any price." The *Cardenio* manuscripts—likely kept from Theobald's Shakespeare by his publisher's need to keep a consistent *Works* for copyright—have long been suspected of belonging to Lot 460. Yet the entry notes that the plays are bound in quarto and makes no mention of an actual manuscript, which would not have been quarto-size but would surely have been the most valuable item in the lot. More likely, Theobald had sold *Cardenio* years earlier to printer John Watts; it is mentioned as remaining in storage as late as 1770 at Covent Garden Playhouse, before the building burned down and left the world one Shakespeare play poorer. But along with the ill-fated *Cardenio*, there was one other curious absence that day from Theobald's auction lots.

Where did his First Folio go?

17 Gough Square, London

THERE ARE NO hours posted outside 17 Gough Square, just a plaque and a yellow paper sign under the window: REPLICA GEORGIAN CLOTHES AVAILABLE FOR CHILDREN TO TRY ON. I can't say I've ever seen any children here. Gough Square is an inconspicuous and tucked-away place; people wander through trying to find the Mediaforce Group or immigration law office. In a different era they might have stopped off here before wandering over to Bream's Buildings, bound for the "sheriff's hotel," where debtors boarded between their arrest and prison. A sensible neighborhood for an author to live in, then: it saved on the commute.

But today it's the last surviving home of Dr. Samuel Johnson. His stout old building is full of faintly absurd bric-a-brac—there's an engraving of "The Infant Johnson" looking uncharacteristically shy, demure, and—of course—chubby. Another room screens a cheerily dorky video of the ghosts of Boswell and Johnson visiting the house today; it loops endlessly, chattering away whether anyone watches or not. Then, towering above it all, is the quiet, reflective mind of the house, the fourth floor: the garret.

I pad upstairs. This garret has been burned-out more than once;

it was bombed three times during the war, including a hit from a V-1 buzz bomb. Other buildings, lacking famous occupants, were not saved; from the garret's window seats you can see where an immense complex of modern glass-and-steel buildings, New Street Square, is going up. At the moment the site looks almost, well, bombed-out.

It would have been in here, in the garret—perhaps over by the long counting-office tables, or among the library shelves. Here: Theobald's old Folio would have been right about here.

If Samuel Johnson remains one of the great stories of London literary life, it is in part because so little predicted it. He was a striking amalgam of gluttony and piety, of quick wit and slow melancholy, of bookishness and brawn. The toweringly tall and muscled son of a Staffordshire bookseller, he was also the nephew of a professional Smithfield boxer and had trained well under him. Boxing might indeed have been his best career in his twenties, as he was an Oxford dropout of mixed prospects at best. After a brief apprenticeship with his father as a bookman, and then going through his wife's money in starting a school—he only attracted three pupils—Johnson trudged to London in 1737 in search of work. His companion for the journey was a promising student of his named David Garrick. Johnson had hopes of writing plays and landing translating work; Garrick had thoughts of becoming a lawyer. The two were something of an odd couple, with Garrick as diminutive, genial, and suave as Johnson was towering, brooding, and subject to violent physical tics; between them they had one horse and took turns walking and riding the 118 miles to the city.

The London they found was newly flooded with cheap copies of Shakespeare, works that were now becoming an object of serious study. Theater managers had already taken notice: stage productions were entering a generation-long peak, a Shakespeare's Ladies Club had just formed, and sentiment was building up for a statue of the bard to be placed in the Poets' Corner of Westminster Abbey.

Johnson was hardly immune to all this: he first chanced upon *Hamlet* as a child of nine, and after reading the ghost scene he'd been so dazed that he ran to the front door, so "that he might see people about him." Now, as a struggling playwright in London, he walked the same streets as his hero once had and rented a cheap room on Catherine and Strand, just steps away from Tonson's bookshop. He'd learned the trick of all scruffy gentlemen in London: sleep in the cheapest room, but linger at respectable coffeehouses. His money was tight, and getting tighter; living on a scant fourpence a day in food, churning out plays and poems and articles, he sometimes slept rough in cellars with his fellow impoverished playwright Richard Savage. Yet even in these dire times, other writers took notice of Johnson. Like Shakespeare, Johnson had an innate and instantaneous capacity for brilliant wit and earthiness; gliding along the Thames, where boaters customarily shouted insults at each other in passing, one luckless stranger received this double-barreled blast back from Johnson: "Sir, your wife, under pretense of keeping a bawdy house, is a receiver of stolen goods."

As for Garrick, law hadn't worked out, and while toiling in his brother's wine business, thoughts of yet another career began to creep over him. Having once acted in a school play for Johnson, he was now visiting Drury Lane to sell wine in the playhouses and was intrigued by what he saw. Loitering with actors at clubs after the shows, he became known for his ability to devastatingly mimic their performances. Yet he was so unsure of his own abilities that when he talked a friendly manager into casting him into some small roles, he played them out of town and under an assumed name. The wine business went to the wayside; he instead became an unknown actor named Mr. Lyddal.

Johnson, too, was slowly finding his place in London. It seems impossible that he would have missed Theobald's estate auction in St. Paul's Coffee-House in 1744; if there was one library in London that Johnson would have longed to possess, it was this one. Whether he could afford to bid on much is another question. Yet, by that day of the auction in 1744, Garrick's and Johnson's lives had both begun to take shape.

After a few bit parts went off well, Garrick was engaged full-time at Drury Lane. Now he was David Garrick by name and an actor by trade. His rookie portrayal of Richard III had made him a name; his King Lear made him a star; his Hamlet made him immortal. The ferocity of his performances was startling; he drew on a new realism that, he explained, came from visiting and studying people in actual distress. To create his Lear, he'd visited a grieving friend who, while dandling his daughter, had fatally dropped her on the flagstone floor of his kitchen—and from that man's endless agonies, Garrick explained, "I copied nature." Audiences noticed: jams of horse-drawn traffic formed in front of the theater whenever he played.

"Garrick," snorted one rival actor, "is a new religion."

And Johnson, after years of praise but little pay from anonymous poetry and magazine articles, finally found acclaim with his newly published *Life of Richard Savage*. His friend had died broke and alone the previous year; and in his biographical memorial, Johnson made a passage from the miseries of obscurity to public regard. Yet he remained so poor that, when a gentleman dined with his publisher to praise the book, Johnson wolfed down food and listened in secret from an adjoining room, too ashamed of his shabby clothes to introduce himself.

Within a few months, though, he had a notion of what he wanted to do with his newfound fame. He was, he decided, to be Shakespeare's next editor.

The year of Theobald's and Pope's deaths had already seen a dramatic development on the London stage. That January, Garrick pointedly advertised that his new production of *Macbeth* was to be "the Tragedy Reviv'd as Shakespeare Wrote it"—no pantomime shows, no clog dances, no modern "improvements." Garrick couldn't help quietly slipping in a few anyway, but the message was clear: the leading actor of his generation had declared that Shakespeare's altar needed no polishing.

Fresh off his life of Savage and in need of money, Johnson also turned to *Macbeth*. In April 1745 he issued his first book of criticism, *Miscellaneous Observations on the Tragedy of Macbeth*; in it, readers found both an astute consideration of the timing of Macbeth's creation—just a few years after King James I had published his volume of *Demonology* against witchcraft—and a careful scene-by-scene disentangling of Shakespeare and his many commentators. Johnson attached to this a single sheet labeled "Proposals for Printing a New Edition of the Plays of William Shakespeare," an ambitious declaration of an upcoming ten-volume octavo edition featuring more commentary. The copyright on Theobald's edition would be running out in a few years, and Johnson was making a grab for the next edition.

It wasn't to be. Jacob Tonson III had in fact picked his next editor—the unmemorable Reverend William Warburton—and he instantly fired off a letter to Johnson's publisher: "As you are a man of character, I had rather satisfy you of our right by argument than by the expense of a Chancery suit." The upstart publisher backed down; Johnson would simply have to wait his turn for Shakespeare. For the intervening decade he turned instead to an even more massive project: *The Dictionary of the English Language*.

It's in this garret that Johnson undertook that task; he'd chosen the room for his library and study because, at four stories up, it's where he was the least likely to get interrupted. Visitors who ventured up these stairs to the top of the building found a room covered in dust, books, papers, and battered furniture. Six assistants compiled entries at long counting tables of the kind typically used in accounting houses, all while Johnson assured his subscribers and his publishers that he'd only need three years to finish it all. Occasionally Johnson excused himself to a side room to amuse himself with a pet project of creating elixirs, though perhaps the chemical reactions got away from him at times: one visitor arrived to find the would-be chemist "all covered with soot like a chimney-sweeper." Explosions might have been a necessary antidote for the glacial pace of his dictionary work: the "three-year" project was six years overdue when Johnson sent the final pages to his publisher in 1755. The unfortunate businessman was heard to mutter, "Thank *God*, I have done with him."

Johnson, as usual, was also done—with the money. The release of a book is a financially perilous time for a writer; one may observe authors, out drinking with friends to celebrate their publication, all the while nervously eyeing the bill and the exit. Johnson's case was even worse, as he'd received his money up front by soliciting subscriptions—a common practice at the time. But that money had come in nearly a decade ago; the praise that the *Dictionary* brought did him no good now. Instead, he found himself mired in depression and poverty, terminating in a note to his friend and fellow writer Samuel Richardson:

I am obliged to entreat your assistance. I am now under arrest for five pounds eighteen shillings.

Had Richardson not brought a few pounds to a bailiff on March 16, 1756—had he, say, been out of town for a while—then English literature might be immeasurably poorer today. Debtor's prison was a miserable, unhealthy place; more than a few writers spent their final hours in it. After his release, Johnson retained a deep disgust that another man could jail him for the lack of five pounds, or indeed for any sum at all. Writing of the common sight of a creditor "whose debtor has perished in prison," he bitterly concluded, "I must leave them to be awakened by some other power; for I write only to human beings." But his own brush with oblivion seemed to galvanize Johnson, for that June he issued a curiously familiar-sounding circular: "Proposals For Printing By Subscription The Dramatic Works of William Shakespeare."

This time, Johnson was ready for the task, and Tonson was ready to hand it to him. He'd matured into an editor who could stroll around Shakespeare's works and view them from many angles—as a scholar, a poet, a playwright, a critic, and a confirmed Londoner. In the preceding decade, not only had Johnson often written on Shakespeare in his *Rambler* essays, he'd also become a playwright himself; Garrick had put on his play *Irene* for a brief run at Drury Lane. Johnson gained a backstage view to the workings of drama, though at length he did stop hanging about Garrick's greenroom.

"I'll no more come behind your scenes, David," he reluctantly admitted, "for the silk stockings and white bosoms of your actresses excite my amorous tendencies."

But now Johnson's work was in dead earnest. He was in such dire need of money that he even sent subscription proposals to old schoolmates to whom he hadn't spoken in twenty years; the wife of painter Joshua Reynolds was so touched that she gamely kept a sheaf of proposals to urge upon her houseguests, until Joshua finally begged her to stop pestering everyone with them. But, at length, the subscriptions did start coming in.

Among those who took notice of Johnson's new project was Dr. Charles Burney, organist of St. Margaret's, eminent musicologist, and writer of what might be called Johnson's first fan letter. An avid reader of Johnson's magazine essays, he'd ventured to write to him two years after the *Dictionary* was published, praising it and subscribing to the new Shakespeare. For all the regard that the *Dictionary* has received throughout history, Johnson had only received miserably hectoring letters upon its publication; then as now, the study of language seems to attract pedants in whom correction becomes the lowest form of learning. The response that Johnson sent to Burney's letter contains one of the most piteous lines in the history of authorship: "Yours is the only letter of goodwill that I have yet received, though I am indeed promised something of that sort from Sweden."

Burney's reward, in the spring of 1758, was a visit with Johnson himself. Johnson, now forty-eight years old, conveyed an overwhelming physical presence upon a first meeting: he was still as towering and broad as in his youth and favored large overcoats that could—and did—contain entire folios in their oversized pockets. His physical tics had remained, too, and to his grimaces and grunts he'd added a squinting nearsightedness. He habitually leaned in too close to his reading light, with the result that his powdered wig was disconcertingly scorched along the brow.

But to Burney, he was welcoming.

The author led Burney up these steps and showed him around

this garret; it was rather less respectably furnished than it appears now. Folios were lying about the floors in a slovenly mess that matched Johnson himself; among them was Theobald's old First Folio, quite possibly procured through the Tonsons. It was this folio that the new editor had at hand while writing on a plain pinewood table. The rest of the room now contained exactly two chairs; or, rather, one and one half. Johnson gave Burney the whole chair, while he sat on a perilously teetering chair with just three legs. He was, he informed Dr. Burney, just months away from finishing the Shakespeare volumes—in fact, they'd be done by the summer. Johnson produced proof sheets to show him the progress being made, and Burney excitedly looked over Johnson's footnotes to *A Merchant of Venice*. They were, Burney noticed aloud, much harder on the most recent editor, Warburton, than on Theobald.

"Oh, poor Tib!" Johnson mused, recalling Pope's satire. "He was [al]ready knocked down . . ."

"But, sir, you'll have Warburton upon your bones, won't you?"

"No, sir, he'll not come out," Johnson said grandly. "He'll only growl in his den."

Burney left delighted with his new friend and cheered by the prospect of receiving his new Shakespeares in a matter of months.

Seven years later, Dr. Burney received his books.

The bare furnishings and broken chair should have been a clue: Johnson had been arrested for debt once again before Burney visited, and this time Tonson had retrieved him. As the summer and then the winter passed with no Shakespeare volumes forthcoming, the moody author received yet another blow—his ninety-year-old mother, whom he adored, had passed away back in Litchfield. He'd missed being at her deathbed—hadn't visited in ages, in fact. His depression might have left him unable to write a word had it not been for his mother's funeral expenses: he bashed out his novella *Rasselas* in a single week, purely to cover her burial fees. The book was so hurried and the author's grief so great that he didn't even read the manuscript through upon finishing it.

Shakespeare was not so easily buried; years passed with nothing to show for it, and people kept asking him about it. When a bookseller's assistant arrived in 1762 with a new subscriber and asked to see the printed subscription list, Johnson finally admitted defeat. "I have two very cogent reasons for not printing any list of subscribers," he explained. "One, that I have lost all the names, — the other, that I have spent all the money." A murmur was beginning to arise, and a pointed squib made the literary rounds: "He for subscribers baits his hook / and takes your cash, but where's the book?"

Johnson's friends agonized over his dire straits; couldn't *something* be done for the country's greatest writer? And something was: to the country's great and everlasting credit, Johnson was awarded a pension by King George III of £300 per year. In time, he would also receive an honorary doctorate from his old college. Dr. Johnson gloried in his new honorific, but was left almost speechless by the pension. This life-altering event was hardly riches, but more than enough for an author to live upon. Johnson had the means and the encouragement to work in earnest upon his Shakespeare once again. By 1765, Burney and other subscribers at last received their prize: a well-edited eight-volume set of Shakespeare.

But what caught the attention of readers was not the plays, but rather Johnson's own preface: here, for the first time, the modern understanding of Shakespeare was born. Alone among Shakespeare's centuries of editors, it is Johnson's introduction that new students of Shakespeare are still invariably given to read today.

What set Shakespeare apart from virtually every other playwright, Johnson pointed out, was that *his plays were not about love.* True, love was a fine thing—"But love is only one of many passions; and as it has no great influence upon the sum of life, it has little operation in the dramas of a poet who caught his ideas from the living world and exhibited only what he saw before him." And true to the world, heroes were difficult to discern in these plays. "Shakespeare has no heroes," Johnson pronounced, "his scenes are occupied only by men." These two elements—a love plot and a central hero—were the veritable oxygen and gravity in the worlds that most playwrights inhabited. But that was not Shakespeare's world. His world was *our* world—and this, Johnson implied, was why Shakespeare had taken his place among the world's great writers.

But if he was a great writer, what was his great book? This, Johnson admitted, had troubled him somewhat; he had dutifully collected a number of early editions, only to find himself doubting the verisimilitude of any except the one folio actually handled by Shakespeare's own players.

"The truth," Johnson announced, "is that the first is equivalent to all others, and that the rest only deviate from it by the printer's negligence . . . I collated them all at the beginning, but afterwards used only the first."

Johnson's timing could not have been more auspicious. Even as his copies were picked up by subscribers, his friend Garrick was hatching a plan to celebrate Shakespeare's two hundredth birthday. With his Stratford Jubilee in September 1769, Garrick presided over four days of unprecedented celebration as Londoners poured into Shakespeare's birthplace: a theater was built on the Avon, a statue erected, banquets thrown, and on Sunday churchgoers paid their

respects at Shakespeare's grave. A parade the next day of Shakespearean characters was only prevented by a sudden storm, but the
banqueting and merriment went on. Gesturing at their new statue,
Garrick announced to the crowd:

"'Tis he! 'Tis he! The god of our idolatry!"

A decade earlier one of Garrick's friends had mused that Shakespeare had become to the English "a kind of established religion in
poetry," but now it was official: Shakespeare was a cultural deity. And
the brilliance of Garrick's festival lay not only in its sheer invention,
but in its public nature. Shakespeare's acclaim as a homegrown genius was transcending his art: one no longer even needed to have
seen a play to take part in celebrating the man. After all, who doesn't
like an excuse for a parade?

Garrick returned to London and continued the celebrations on
Drury Lane, but his jubilee in Stratford never really ended. Before,
minor towns and cities were toured only for their religious significance or their curative powers. But now Stratford became England's
first place of purely manufactured secular pilgrimage: in short, our
first real tourist trap. Shakespeare editions, Shakespeare souvenirs,
Shakespeare prints and paintings—a Shakespeare idolatry developed,
so pronounced that pilgrims sought out slivers from the mulberry
tree he'd supposedly planted and bought up entire neighborhoods'
worth of Shakespeare's old furniture.

Garrick and Johnson might have stood together and admired
their handiwork, if only they hadn't been so annoyed with each other.
Johnson had never been in awe of Garrick; he knew him too well
and too long and could effortlessly puncture his friend by guffawing
backstage during some particularly touching scene. But in private,
Johnson complained that Garrick hadn't picked up any book subscriptions among his friends and hadn't loaned him old plays from

his library. One could hardly blame Garrick, though; Johnson had a reputation for being as careless with books as he was with everything else about his person.

Decades earlier, as an obscure Litchfield schoolmaster, Johnson had been asked by Mrs. Garrick what he thought of her son. "Why, madam," he replied, "David will either be hanged, or become a great man." Now both had achieved greatness, and in their own inimitable ways—one through dramatic spectacle, and the other through patient scholarship—they'd also brought forth a beatification. In thirty years, Garrick and Johnson had gone from two unemployed young men walking into London to the country's first cultural kingmakers. In their hands, Shakespeare had become a national saint—and the First Folio his one true book.

Staple Inn, High Holborn, London

STAPLE INN IS the sole survivor of London's nine old Inns of Chancery, and its archway by Chancery Lane tube remains remarkably inconspicuous. Nathaniel Hawthorne once blundered through the very same entrance, and discovered this wide courtyard of oak trees, old flagstones, gently chiming bells upon the hour, and a stillness so intense that he could hear the bees humming among the courtyard's shrubbery. "There was not a quieter spot in England than this," he marveled. "In all the hundreds of years since London was built, it has not been able to sweep its roaring tide over that little island of quiet."

The island remains, for I have the courtyard to myself as I sit on its octagonal bench and stare at its office windows. For four hundred years London lawyers worked in buildings like this one: high ceilinged, spacious, and whitewashed, with tall windows that spoke of prosperity. And each morning in the final decades of the 1700s, as this courtyard's bells chimed seven, George Steevens strolled in on his mission from Hampstead. Steevens always began his rounds of the city here, in office number 1, with an earnest editing of Shakespeare in the chambers of his friend Isaac Reed. At times Steevens would show up so early in the morning—at two A.M., even—that Reed simply left the key out for him. But the learned attorney was one of Steevens's few equals among London's Shakespeare scholars, and the only one with no interest in self-aggrandizement.

"I have such a horror of seeing my name as Author or Editor," Reed once explained, "that if I had the option of standing in the pillory, or standing before the publick in either of those lights, I should find it difficult to determine which to choose."

Steevens was of a more ambitious stamp. The well-heeled son of a director of the East India Company, Steevens's professional interest in Shakespeare dated back to his youth, when he'd served as an assistant in Samuel Johnson's garret. The Doctor passed the editorial line of succession on to him, and for years Steevens would follow his sunrise discussion at Reed's office with a visit to his mentor; sometimes Johnson would make the return trip and take tea here in Reed's chambers. But those days were gone. Now Steevens instead paused to look at a curious memento: the timepiece that Johnson had once carried, engraved by the Doctor's old friends in the watchmaking Mudge family. It had become Steevens's after Dr. Johnson's death in 1784. After leaving Reed's, Steevens would stop by the Mudge shop, just as Johnson had, and set the exact minutes and hours on his old friend's watch.

Then, with a few more social calls and his watch set, it was time for the real work of his day to begin: buying books.

I walk down the Strand popping a coin back and forth between my hands, then pausing to observe it; I'd be sorry to lose it, but it's not as if I can spend it anywhere around here. It's a massy bit of copper, the size of an American quarter, but not in any modern denomination; nor is it of any government treasury. It's a book token. The obverse side bears the date 1795, while the reverse is struck with the figure of the three Muses and encircled with two lines:

HALFPENNY OF JAMES LACKINGTON,
ALLEN & CO.
GREATEST BOOKSTORE IN THE WORLD

That was no idle boast.

London in the final years of the eighteenth century was a glorious place to buy books. The country's first modern book-dealer, James Lackington, had built a shop so grandly laid out that he could—and did—drive a horse-drawn carriage all the way around its interior. An uneducated shoemaker who taught himself the book trade after beginning in 1774 with a mere five pounds' worth of books from his own bookshelf, Lackington kept prices down ruthlessly with high-volume, cash-only sales; he mastered the dark arts of remaindering and store layout, cannily placing cheaper books in the upper reaches of his cathedral-domed store, while displaying his bibliophilic riches at the front counter of his self-proclaimed "Temple of the Muses." For all the shop's grandeur, Lackington possessed a brilliant understanding of how to cater to even the wealthiest buyers' desire to believe they'd purchased a bargain. He regularly sold books to pawnbrokers, who flipped them at inflated prices to unwary "purchasers believing that they are buying bargains, and that such articles have been pawned."

Some pawnshop bargains, of course, really were just a little too good to be legit. Charles Burney Jr.—the son of Dr. Johnson's greatest fan—was caught at Cambridge purloining books from the university library to pay for his gambling habit. He'd stolen nearly a hundred volumes by the time he was caught with the latest haul in his dorm room. Burney rather elegantly chose easily palmed sixteenth-century Elzevir octavos to steal, but good taste hardly weighed in his favor: he was instantly expelled, and his father had very nearly disowned him. A boy getting into trouble at college is not so surprising; what is remarkable, though, is that London now had a market valuing old books enough that Burney could go drinking and dicing off the proceeds.

Steevens, on the other hand, kept booksellers honest. Walking about each day with a nosegay of flowers tied dashingly to the head of his cane, he was as experienced at buying books as Lackington was at selling them. And by the 1780s, he started noticing something curious about Shakespeare's 1623 Folio: copies were turning up where booksellers had cannibalized old Folios for parts to "fix" an incomplete volume. Sometimes the pages were from other First Folios; other times the pages were from Second, Third, or Fourth Folios. Others didn't even bother finding the replacement pages: they simply forged them.

"When leaves have been wanting," Steevens complained, "they had been reprinted with battered types, and foisted into the vacancies, without notice."

The title page, with its iconic Droeshout portrait, seemed particularly liable to this kind of chicanery. It was common for Folios to lack them; now it was becoming common to restore them through subterfuge. "When the title has been lost, a spurious one has been fabricated," Steevens warned, "with a blank space left for the head of Shakespeare, afterwards added from a second, third, or fourth impressions." Some didn't come from any Folio at all; sellers created *hand-drawn* look-alike portraits in some Folios.

What, exactly, was going on here?

· · ·

Where Strand meets Catherine Street, the intersection is one of dueling crews. Over at the Novello Theatre, union men are loading in a new production of *A Midsummer Night's Dream*; while across the street, hard hatters are steadily demolishing a building, bludgeoning it with iron claws into a twisted mass of dirt, dust, rebar, and smashed brick. The site was once the home of the Leigh & Sotheby auction house. Books that began their life on this corner at Tonson's would eventually return to begin life all over again across the street, a bit cheaper and worse for wear.

But something curious was happening with the 1623 Folios. Buoyed with Garrick's and Johnson's praise, by the 1750s First Folios began to be worth *more* than their original price of one pound: they crossed the border from used book to collectible. The gains were modest; as late as the 1780s, it was possible to find a Folio for two pounds, less even than what new collected editions cost. But change was afoot. Folios turned up on the front page of bookseller catalogs, and owners were hiring book restorers at several pounds a pop to fix their old Folios.

The breaking point came in an auction room on March 2, 1790; tucked among a number of other antiquarian treasures, the auction catalog listed a 1604 *Hamlet* quarto of which "no other copy is known to exist." Steevens was having none of it; while his rivals bid up the quarto, he claimed to know where to find two more copies. In fact, just to rub it in, he claimed that he had one himself. Even so, the *Hamlet* took down an extraordinary £17—far more than any of the previous 364 lots, most of which went for just a few shillings. The crowd had barely caught its breath when bidding on a particularly fine copy of the First Folio also rocketed upward—five pounds? Ten? Twenty?—until a worried buying agent signaled his client, the Duke of Roxburghe, who was watching from among the spectators.

The Folio was reaching unheard-of prices, and did he want to keep bidding? The Scottish nobleman already had a Folio, after all.

Roxburghe penciled in a reply: *Lay on, Macduff—And damned be he who first cries, "Hold, enough!"*

The duke walked out triumphantly with a £34 Folio under his arm—a year's wages for some—and so pleased with his new Folio that he grandly made a gift of his old one to his buying agent. From that day forward the Folio, Steevens marveled, "would now become the most expensive single book in our language."

And where there is money, there is fakery: patch-up jobs and fac-simile leaves become inevitable. Authenticity was a tricky subject for Steevens, though, as he himself was exceedingly fond of hoaxes. Never one to suffer fools, Steevens nonetheless delighted in *making* them. Over the years, he'd created a fake chapter from an Eastern epic, purely to fool one of his friends; he'd planted a magazine story of a "poisonous Upas tree" of Java that killed anything within a fifteen-mile radius; and he bedeviled the head of the Society of An-tiquaries with both a forged (and insulting) book inscription, and by commissioning a fake seven-hundred-year-old Saxon tombstone to King Hardicanute. The latter Steevens planted it in the window of a Kensington Lane curio shop, where he knew his mark would spot it. Steevens patiently waited for his victim to write an entire illustrated journal article on his "discovery" before gleefully revealing his ruse.

But Shakespeare was no joking matter to Steevens. Working alongside Johnson while the good Doctor had written his preface, Steevens had come to the same conclusions about the Folios. The Third and Fourth Folios, Steevens sniffed, "are little better than waste paper," though the early quartos were worth consulting. But "of all the other plays," he decided, "the only authentick edition is the folio of 1623."

Not long after the duke of Roxburghe's extravagant purchase, Steevens had become dubious about the prices being fetched: he spurned a Folio offered to him for £21. But then again, he didn't really need that Folio. Dr. Johnson's watch wasn't the only reminder of his old friend that he'd kept.

"Here it is," a curator tells me.

The book is laid on the table in front of me with a faint *whump*: a Folio bound in brown sheepskin, its front hinge cracking a bit, and the royal seal of lion and unicorn: *Dieu et mon droit.*

"This is the Steevens?"

"This is the Steevens."

I nod as he paces back across the long expanse of the Rare Book Room. I am seated, rather incongruously, in front of a burly British Library staffer at the Music Enquiries desk.

"Hello," I say cheerily.

He does not respond.

Music Enquiries is the counter closest to any reading desk, and thus the spot they reserve for terrifyingly rare volumes. While other patrons in Rare Books—where pens are banned, and security examines your goods in clear plastic bags coming and going—are allowed to keep teetering stacks of old books at their desks when they leave, this desk is different. The deal is that if I step away from it, they immediately examine the book and whisk it away. Getting it back takes going through the entire request process again. So: no breaks, no sudden movements, nothing allowed on the desk but paper and pencil. At no time is the book to be left unattended.

"Well," I mutter to myself. "Here we are."

Opening it up, I find a leaf inserted with a note in Steevens's crisp handwriting:

<u>Shakespeare,</u>

<u>Folio, 1623</u>

G. STEEVENS. Ex dono Jacobi Tonson, bibiop. 1765.

It belonged to Mr. Theobald.

From him it devolved to Dr. Johnson,

who did not much improve its condition.

Which is putting it mildly. Paging through the comedies at the front of the volume, I find that although the book has the usual ink drips and burn flecks, it also has a remarkable number of . . . well, *food stains*. Garrick's hesitation to loan his old books to Dr. Johnson is starting to make lots of sense. There are greasy fingerprints on *A Midsummer Night's Dream*, an unidentifiable smear across the second act of *A Merchant of Venice*, and a crescent-shaped ring across the front of *Measure for Measure* that is so clearly from a tea saucer that it should be a permanent exhibit in the Doctor Johnson Gallery of Bad Housekeeping.

And I'm pretty sure that Samuel had a taste for gravy.

But here's what he did not have a taste for: histories. Johnson claimed that there were only really two kinds of Shakespeare plays—comedies and tragedies. He meant that the histories could be divided among the others; and yet, he clearly had less interest in the history plays themselves. His regard is tangible, for as I get further into the Folio and into the histories—past the strange sprinklings over the closing pages of *Twelfth Night*—the paper gets noticeably *cleaner*. Whiter. It's not crisp, exactly; I have found that the old linen paper in Folios is surprisingly soft. I'm not sure that it's possible to get a paper cut from it; you might as well try to cut yourself with a dishrag. Yet the histories do feel different under my fingertips; the pages that Johnson only occasionally visited have a tactile difference.

And then, just as the tragedies begin again: more gravy.

To be fair, maybe it's not all Dr. Johnson. Along with Theobald, Steevens, and the Tonsons, there was also a whole unknown first century of owners; maybe some squire dropped his eel pie on this front page of *Romeo and Juliet*. Nor, for that matter, were Johnson and Steevens the final owners. Still another signature is in the front endpapers: *Charles Burney, D D Deptford*. The felonious young Burney had, of all things, reinvented himself as a doctor of divinity and—parlaying his precocious expertise at book acquisition into more legitimate methods—had bid £22 for this Folio after Steevens's estate was sold off in a ten-day Covent Garden bibliomaniacal blowout auction. A decade later, Burney himself would be the deceased party, and much of his own library would be disposed in precisely the same way at the Leigh & Sotheby's on Catherine Street.

Each owner has left his mark. One of them removed the Droeshout portrait; subsequent owners inserted two to replace it. Steevens, a talented amateur artist, even amused himself by hand-sketching a replacement Droeshout that is curiously smooth and serene; lacking the cross-hatching of the original, it almost makes the bard look as if he were wearing eyeliner. And sometime after the library aquired this volume in 1818, it had it rebound; the original owners wouldn't even recognize it on a shelf anymore. Yet for all its many owners, this folio still feels like Johnson's. The pages of the Doctor's favored tragedies—*Othello*, *King Lear*, *Hamlet*—are all conspicuously darker and dirtier than the rest of the folio, and his beloved *Macbeth* is grubbiest of all. After Steevens received this book from Johnson, he could only marvel at the reading habits of his predecessors.

"They fed and studied at the same instant," he mused. "I have repeatedly met *thin* flakes of *pie-crust* between leaves of our author."

Steevens then drolly suggests that Shakespeare's artistry was so overwhelming that readers literally went slack-jawed—and out fell their food.

But something about these pages *is* physically moving—and not just because it is Shakespeare. This is the volume that Theobald peered into as creditors hounded him; these are the lines of type where Johnson sought solace as he wrestled the lonely silence that greeted his *Dictionary*; in these endpapers Steevens scratched his comments before making his great circuits of the city; in these marginal notes Burney saw the memorial of his father's generation, whose history was now passing away before his eyes. Books bear a tangible presence alongside their ineffable quality of thought: they have a body and a soul. All the books in this room do. And so here—the lights buzzing far overhead, the guard scowling, the cool wood of the desk under my fingers, and the softened and smudged pages of *Lear* before me—lies this same folio, bearing mute witness to the overwhelming fact behind every salesroom that it has ever passed through: our books will outlive us.

ACT III

Charing Cross, London

CHARING CROSS TODAY only bears a few stalwart remainders from its once-mighty book trade; now it's piss-ups, theaters, and Topper's £6 Haircuts. In the window of Henry Pordes, thank goodness, I can still find a loony old title like *The Romance of the London Directory*. Actually, not so loony, according to author Rev. Charles Bardsley: "I find as much pleasure in perusing these directories as any schoolgirl over her first and most sensational novel." Fair enough: all book collectors have their curious obsessions. And if the Folio was yours, then for many years just a few streets were really worth haunting, and they're all near Charing Cross.

Charing Cross runs to the north, and the Strand to the east; think of Trafalgar Square as the wishbone. Along Strand you had Henry Sotheran by Sotheby's old digs, with the sons of book patriarch Uriah Maggs taking up shop in No. 109. Charing Cross put you by Henry Rodd's store on Great Newport and Joseph Lilly's shop on King Street; not too far to the west were the shops of Bernard Quaritch and Pickering & Chatto. For much of the nineteenth century, you could take a stroll in a single hour among these shops and be apprised of the existence and price of probably every First Folio for sale in Britain—and perhaps in the world.

Sotheran, Maggs, and Quaritch have all moved farther afield since then; Lilly and Rodd are simply gone. At the end of the block from Pordes, I cut over to the corner and down Great Newport, to where Rodd's old storefront is now occupied by the remains of the Long Island Ice Tea Shop. The windows are papered over with failure— London apparently lacks a sufficient sorority demographic—but even as workmen tear out fittings to make way for the next transitory business, you can still see the outlines of what would have been Rodd's store.

Of course, only a Lilly or a Rodd would actually have made a circuit and kept track of every Folio: who bought them, where to find them, what condition they were in, who needed to sell for cash, and who had an estate coming up. Such knowledge existed in the minds and sales-book jottings of canny book dealers; no one would actually *track* such things. Except that for a time in the 1800s, that's exactly what one boyish and unassuming clergyman walking these streets did.

Past the royal-mail postboxes and the black-clad taxi queue, the Charing Cross concourse has that distinct sound of rail stations, of steps ricocheting endlessly between marble floors and lattice-vaulted skylights; commuters check the white-on-blackboards before scurrying to platform 4, to 7, to 2, to whichever way into or out of the city, all while balancing scalding Nero cups and that morning's *Metro*.

HEADCORN reads my ticket. Platform 5.

Once I've settled in on the Margate via Canterbury train, I reach into my backpack and pull out a coverless old octavo in tatters: the second volume of Dibdin's *The Library Companion: Or, The Young*

Man's Guide and The Old Man's Comfort in the Choice of a Library. Though not so nicely bound as the copy I saw back at Sotheby's, its sentiments remain unchanged by the beating it's taken over the last two centuries. Writing in 1824, the Reverend Thomas Dibdin found London on the verge of a new and extraordinary era of bibliophilia; even as he was writing this volume, Lackington's Temple of the Muses was boasting a staggering twenty-seven-thousand-volume catalog, and another local bookseller had rakishly taken out a *thousand*-line ad in the *Times* classifieds.

Amid all the moneyed speculation in the book market, Thomas Dibdin himself was a curious sort of outsider. An orphan raised by his great-aunt in the 1780s, Dibdin was left with a schoolmaster fond of buying castoffs by the sack-load from book dealers. The boy's imagination was captured by the piles of remainders and foxed volumes, and he enthusiastically wrote three plays at the age of fourteen and anxiously gave them to his aunt to read; later, "receiving the bedchamber candle from the servant, I found a piece of paper at the bottom of the candle, to keep it steady in the stick, upon which my handwriting was but too visible." She had been using his plays for wastepaper—and thus ended his stage career.

I look up: the train is taking an elevated line out of London, so that we glide past the fourth floors of innumerable office buildings: workers and computers are visible through the greenish windows of conference rooms—including one office that, alarmingly, appears to have a skeleton hanging in the middle of the room. I gawk a moment, and the scene slides past, anonymous, into an endless series of cubicles.

It was these people—the toilers and the strivers like himself—that Dibdin so often addressed. True, he moved easily among the nobility; after taking a respectable if unremunerative calling in the ministry, Dibdin was a founding member in 1812 of the Roxburghe Club, which came about spontaneously when collectors dined together the night before the estate auction of that great and rash buyer of Folios. Yet Dibdin's pay from the collection plate hardly matched that of the lords that he dined with. A spectator more than a collector, Dibdin spent many hours in the libraries of his noble friends; the digs of Thomas Grenville, an MP and Lord of the Admiralty, were a special favorite of his. Grenville had a twenty-thousand-volume collection filled with only the most flawless and rare volumes. It wasn't enough for Grenville to have one of only two copies of a 1506 Italian travelogue in India: he had to have the *flawless* copy of the two.

"Not only for its dimensions . . . have I never *seen* anything like it," Dibdin marveled of Grenville's library, "but I can have *no conception* of anything going beyond it."

These were books, Dibdin explained, so shatteringly rare that they simply could not be bought—"unless on the death of a very prominent collector." Dibdin's hours among these rare and curious volumes culminated in this volume in my hands. But the greatest curiosity within the *Library Companion*'s pages is not any priceless octavo or Renaissance travel, nor the hundreds of pages of polyglot Bibles or Holinshed folios and books of martyrs. It is by Dibdin himself—and he has hidden it in the subterranean world of his footnotes.

Tonbridge, Paddock Wood, Marden: the stations slip by and merge into placid fields of sheep. There is, improbably, a trampoline in the middle of one of these paddocks—as if bouncing children had been assigned to keep sentinel over the country's rail lines. It would hardly be the oddest notion I've come across today.

The Library Companion was a thousand-page ramble amid the peaks of British collecting, squarely between the speculative bubble of Dibdin's 1809 paean, *Bibliomania,* and the market crash of his 1832 guide, *Bibliophobia*, when cholera and political upheaval were emptying out auction houses. The book today is largely a forgotten curiosity—but I prop the second volume on my train table and leaf to the back, pausing over a long footnote beginning halfway down page 817. It is one that, from its first lines, seems to know that it will outlive all the surrounding text.

"Of all the NOTES, in this *noteable* volume, the present is one which will probably afford the most general interest and amusement . . . ," Dibdin says, warming to his subject. "I am about to make mention of THIRTY COPIES (described in a manner more or less circumstantial) of the first folio of 1623."

What Dibdin had done—what nobody else had ever done before—was ask a question that is almost childlike in its pure simplicity. *Where do books go after they get sold?* To figure that out, you'd have to track down each copy. And so he began walking around London to find them. His first impulse—naturally, for an Englishman—was to separate what he found into classes.

"CLASS THE FIRST," a line proclaims: "These have the size, condition, and the genuine properties of a true copy . . . They have no spurious leaves foisted in from other editions—and are 'sound to the back bone.'" Such Folios were already a rarity after two centuries, though his friend Lord Grenville had one. Dibdin found Grenville's so "beautifully bound" that he was moved to note that it cost Grenville "the sum of £121 16s: the highest price ever given, or likely to be given, for the volume."

(cough)

Very well, then.

If you are to have a first class, you must also have a *second*, and so

Dibdin obliges us. Under "CLASS THE SECOND," his footnote lays out those Folios with a few replacement pages, a gravy stain or two, and those cut down for rebinding to a mere 8 1/8 inches wide, say, instead of a full and glorious 8 1/2. The duke of Roxburghe had been perfectly happy to acquire just such a second-class copy.

For those to be banished even further downward, Dibdin reserves "CLASS THE THIRD"—a category he immediately defines with "the copy in the British Museum belonging to the late Dr. Burney; [and] that in the Dissenter's Library [of Dr. Williams]." The copies at Sotheby's and the British Library may be priceless today, but their marked-up and finger-stained leaves once landed them near the bottom of the Folio heap. But this was where most Folios lay, as Dibdin's long list of such third-class owners even includes . . . well, King George.

On and on the details roll under my fingers—who owned them and where, how much they paid, until the footnotes actually take over entire pages. Without really meaning to, Dibdin became the first man to author a book census: Shakespeare's First Folio, alone among all books, is the only one whose individual copies we can consistently trace back through the nineteenth and often well into the eighteenth or even seventeenth century.

Yet even as Dibdin took a boyish delight in rare books, not even the collectors could maintain such utter belief in the worth of what they were buying. The speculative bubble around old books burst in the 1830s: libraries of tens of thousands of volumes slid precipitously into estate auctions at diminished prices. "Book-madness, like fashions in dress, was carried beyond the verge of the ridiculous," mused one London journalist afterward, "and in it Dibdin was the Beau Brummell of the folly."

Perhaps, but he was still living on the pay of a clergyman. Dibdin's reading was in the libraries of his friends, and his collecting vicari-ous; he was constantly pressed into borrowing even to pay for neces-sities. In his later years, his writings dwindled down to notes begging for a few pounds, with one letter in 1845 asking to borrow money for a holiday turkey. When he died in 1847, the Reverend Thomas Dibdin—a man who'd handled hundreds of thousands of pounds' worth of books in life—had scarcely enough money left to even get buried. Like Theobald and Johnson and countless other antiquarians, Dibdin spent his life surrounded by riches while mired in poverty.

Dibdin's love of books was profoundly and artlessly sincere: he stood to gain nothing by it and took a pure delight in Folios. Where could one even hope to find such a man today?

"Headcorn," the conductor announces.

High Halden, Kent

HEADCORN'S A PENSIVE spot from which to watch a train pull away: it used to be possible to continue onward into the valley, and I can see the old disused platform for its Rother Valley branch line. It overlooks nothing and leads nowhere. The line dried up after the war, its rails torn up for scrap, and villagers here have spent decades slowly reacquiring the line in what seems a very slow-motion rendition of *The Titfield Thunderbolt*. So far they've laid a few hundred yards of rail.

"High Halden," I tell a cabbie, and we flee into the Kentish countryside. You will not have heard of the town: it is so obscure that an 1878 *Guide to the County of Kent* gives it scarcely more than a single sentence, noting that it was "principally celebrated in medieval times for its bad roads." It has not changed much: we get lost in the Wealden forests—a stretch also once celebrated for witchcraft trials—and stray helplessly to the local seat of Harbourne Hall before I finally phone and beg for directions.

There are estates here recorded in the Domesday Book, and property lines dating to the Battle of Hastings, but yet it remains a wonder that Harbourne or any other hall was ever built; so miserable and muddy was the village that the crown itself finally had to sue for it to build some access to the outside world. The traveler William Henry Ireland damned High Halden and its handful of inhabitants in 1830 with the blunt assessment that the village was "very retired, damp and as unpleasant as any I have seen within the county."

But perhaps he is not to be trusted. In a previous career, after all, Ireland had made his name by forging Shakespeare manuscripts—a task assisted in no small part by the First Folio that his family possessed. The fate of his copy is, alas, now unknown—and the one man who might find it again now lives in the very village that Ireland once despised.

We find the house nearly hidden among the lanes, with cords of wood stacked high on its porch and a slight mist over the pond and fields that stretch off into thickly wooded Weald of Kent. I'm ushered to the back of a bright and airy modern home, with glass walls, octagonal skylights, cedar shingles, and a back deck. It precisely resembles the gentrifying homes of Marin County from the 1970s, and what a home like this is doing in the Weald is unfathomable: it's an utter anomaly here, and indeed anywhere in Britain. But its resident—a seventy-five-year-old man convalescing in a rumpled gray sweater and brown corduroys—is no less extraordinary. He is Anthony James West—the single most successful finder of Folios the world has ever known.

"So you found us!" Dr. West calls in greeting from his chair. Perhaps it's the stiff posture of being laid up from knee surgery, but if you didn't know better, you'd think West was an old military officer; he's precisely the sort of fellow you'd have Geoffrey Palmer play.

Here he's among his books, a laptop computer whirring away, and a contented black Lab sprawled out by his feet on a Persian rug. "Don't mind Poppy there, she's a friendly sort."

The dog affirms this with a few thumps of her tail on the rug, then again dozes off. I can't help craning my neck up to the vaulted ceiling, even as I sit down.

"You know," I begin, "I used to live in Sausalito, and this house is uncanny. How on earth did you find a building like this in England?"

"Ah, well." He smiles. "There's a simple explanation. I built it. I wanted something similar to the houses I'd been to in California."

"You used to live there?"

"I spent time in a great many places, back in my consulting days."

"I was curious about that. How did business consulting lead to Folios?"

His wife, Serena, slips in to bring us tea, and he carefully accepts his cup.

"Consulting and books have always gone together for me," he says, and pauses to sip his tea. "My father was a letterpress printer, so I was brought up around the smell of ink. But I didn't really get an education in old books until I went to the States for Harvard Business School."

"That's not the path I would have guessed."

"Curious, isn't it? But I worked with William Jackson back then, the director of the Houghton Library—he's who taught me bibliography. A *complete* contrast from the business school classes."

"How so?"

"In business you learn strategy. What are your values? What are your strengths and weaknesses?" Scholarship, he says, isn't so pointedly fast or competitive. "Jackson, for instance, was the editor of the second edition of the *Short Title Catalogue*. You've seen it?"

Indeed I have. The *Short Title Catalogue* is one of those books that patrons see at every library reference desk without knowing what it is: a bedrock of literary study, and a guide to every publication, publisher, and real and fictive place imaginable.

"That was an *immense* undertaking," West agrees. It was, in fact, precisely the sort of literary cathedral-building that outlives its planners. Jackson, whose brilliance as a rare-book collector for Harvard earned him the nickname the Grand Acquisitor, died years before he could see any of the *STC*'s three revised volumes published. But to West, the task that Jackson had set for himself was justified by his ample talents. "That sort of work requires patience, accuracy, and an in-depth understanding of a field and its resources."

It's a description that sounds rather familiar, particularly when you see the subtitle of the book in my backpack: *A New Worldwide Census of First Folios.* It's not the Dibdin: for there are *two* books in my backpack. This one is by Anthony James West, Ph.D., and it has become his life's work.

"Not many books have had censuses," West admits. In fact, a census of censuses would be a short task: there's the Folio, the Gutenberg Bible, Audubon's *Birds of America*, Copernicus's *De Revolutionibus*, and Darwin's *Origin of Species.* That's it; and four of those five originated in the last few decades. Only the Folio's tally stretches across the centuries, and it has become more ambitious with each iteration; West's ongoing study, *The Shakespeare First Folio: The History of the Book*, may qualify him as the most indefatigable pursuer of a single edition in literary history.

"I've been at it since 1990," he muses. He's published two of five projected volumes with Oxford University Press; the first charts the ups and downs (mostly ups) of what people have been willing to pay for a First Folio, while the second tracks the ownership of each copy over the centuries. At his current rate, he'll finish his project when he turns eighty-five.

"How did it get started?"

"I still remember the moment. It started over there." He points to a sofa by the fireplace. "It was in 1989, and I was sitting right there, reading. Paul Werstine had an article—in the *Library*, have you seen it?—where he talked about uncataloged Folios sitting at the Folger Library. *Uncataloged.* They'd acquired them almost a century before, and they didn't know what they had! There was a desperate need for a census."

"But you were consulting back then?"

"I had been—after getting my M.B.A. in 1958, I consulted up into the eighties. Essentially my job was to bring American know-how to Europe. The sort of analysis that Robert McNamara had done. I was working with Raytheon, IT and T, VW—I even became a partner at Booz Allen." He pauses and looks out over the fields. "I wish I'd spent less time in business."

"Soured on it?"

"Oh, no, no! That was the problem. I loved it, *loved* it. I was taking jobs in Brazil and North Africa! It was tremendous fun for a young man. Every company had new problems, new products, new things to learn. But it made me come to the project late."

He found that every generation or two since Dibdin had seen some sort of attempt at chronicling the Folio. After the thirty-copy listing in 1824, bookseller Henry Bohn had raised it to thirty-nine in 1863, and a group of *Notes and Queries* magazine readers made it to fifty by 1897. These casual efforts were, though, thrown into shadow by British critic Sidney Lee in 1902 with the world's first comprehensive census: he printed up a questionnaire that he sent out to hundreds of libraries and possible Folio owners and tripled the known number to 158 copies.

But it didn't stop there.

"Within a month of its publication," Lee later wrote, "three owners, who failed to communicate with me earlier, wrote to me of copies which had escaped my observation." Others followed, and by 1906 Lee's census had climbed to 172 copies. And there, with some additions by other scholars over the years, is where things stood for the next century or so until a British business consultant curled up on a sofa and opened his new issue of the *Library*.

West has his own number to tell me.

"Two hundred and thirty," he says.

Two hundred and thirty copies: that's how many known First Folios there are now. Folios have been found in Africa and in Australia; there are Folios across Europe and Asia and America. Incredibly, West has personally seen nearly all of them. Their owners are a varied lot—from a Microsoft billionaire to a bucolic Irish college—and all seem to have welcomed West's quest. One owner even let him take a copy back to his hotel to examine it. West assures owners they may remain private, if they wish.

"One owner only wanted to be identified by the continent he was on," he says, "and I honored that wish."

There are only two copies he hasn't yet viewed—and he adds, "I expect to see those on my next visits."

"You're still looking?"

"I've nearly spent my life savings on this," he says a bit ruefully. "A fucking *fortune*."

· · ·

At the moment, fresh from the Wellington Hospital, he's not in a position to start booking flights. Yet there are always more copies to find, more to seek out, and he must prioritize carefully.

"It's becoming a function of age," he says plainly.

Even at 230 copies, the number is liable to keep creeping upward. West has another 130 leads—some, he says, are "quite hot." Newly discovered Folios *do* still turn up. One incident in 2004 reads like a fairy tale: A homemaker living near Manchester was startled to be named the sole surviving relative of a late cousin she'd never heard of before; among the elderly recluse's effects was a Folio that executors listed as "presumed to be a facsimile edition." It was, in fact, the real thing—and a previously unknown copy.

Usually, though, it's the experts who have their eyes out for these copies. An Exeter bookseller in the 1930s scooped up a Folio in a cheap and anonymous binding for just a few shillings as part of a junk lot at an estate sale, and West himself later discovered another Folio in the Yorkshire mining town of Skipton. The book had been mislabeled after a rebinding job in 1936 and then forgotten. Others briefly reveal themselves before disappearing again into tantalizing mysteries. There have been rumors since 1923 of a Folio in New Delhi, and in 1956 another surfaced in the Siberian town of Tomsk before disappearing. Foreigners were not even allowed into the city until 1994; any investigator will now face a trail that has been going cold since the days of *Sputnik*.

Some trails seem to descend in an underbrush of sales and estates and rebinding; others go right off a cliff. Take Folios #157 and #158 from the Lee list: they do not even have West numbers, and indeed only nominally possessed their Lee numbers. Number 158 was lost in the Great Chicago Fire of 1871, while #157 was caught up in another disaster with even more appalling circumstances. New York lawyer

Aldon W. Griswold bought it and shipped it from Liverpool on September 22, 1854, on the SS *Arctic*, a sumptuous luxury steamship famed as one of the fastest boats in the North Atlantic. Too fast, in fact: it plunged into a fogbank off Newfoundland and rammed a French steamer. When survivors began turning up on land, there was a suspicious preponderance of crew members—thirty-two of them, versus only eleven passengers. The *Arctic*'s crew had panicked as their boat sank, drunkenly rushing the lifeboats and shoving passengers into the water. Some two hundred and fifty passengers died in the melee, including all of the women and children on board.

And Griswold, despite going on to become one of America's greatest Shakespeare collectors, never did buy another First Folio after that.

Dr. West hobbles over to his printer, then hands me a sheaf. "Here's the project. All five volumes."

His wife and I are at a table lunching on cold ham, and between bites I feel my eyebrows rising higher and higher as I scan over the prospectus. Although the Folio census began as a doctoral dissertation for the University of London, West has expanded his task into a project so monumental as to almost defy belief.

"I wish I'd applied for academic funding," he admits, though perhaps it is better for the world that he did not. He might never have tried in the face of the discouragement that he would surely have received from any funding officer. Nobody in his right mind would have thought in 1989 that a retired corporate consultant could undertake one of the world's greatest feats of bibliography. And any sensible academic would have broken it down into publishable nuggets—a flood of articles—thinly slicing their findings into what tenure-minded profs jokingly refer to as "least publishable units."

No, a project this vast in scope and ambition could only have been dreamed up—and carried out—by an amateur sitting on a sofa in the English countryside.

West will soon become the first person outside of Jaggard's print shop to have seen every known Folio.

It goes even further than that. The planned third volume will examine Folios and record details of *every page of every copy*. When completed, it will definitely—and, I suspect, permanently—make the First Folio the most scrutinized book edition in the history of written language. But, he claims, it's getting easier as he goes along.

"It's like a detective coming to his tenth murder," he muses. "You start to discern patterns and common approaches."

This time around, he says, he's using a systems analyst to develop a spreadsheet matrix with one axis for each of the Folio's nine hundred pages, and the other axis for parameters ranging from textual variants and marginal markings to repairs and watermarks. Each Folio gets its own spreadsheet, with thousands of cells of information; the aggregated mass of 230 Folio spreadsheets will encompass *millions* of cells of information.

"And you don't worry about"—I pause delicately—"the time involved?"

"Oh, certainly. But I've been working with Eric Rasmussen at the University of Colorado, as well as grad students. The project can outlast me."

If it does, they will have their work cut out for them. Volumes four and five will entail a history of the Folio and an intensely detailed study of paper and conservation.

"There has been nothing on watermarks," West remarks between bites. "They were noted—radiographs were made—but that's all we know."

Studying a book down to the very fibers of its being would seem the logical extension of the task West has begun. His researchers will be equipped with a light-sheet, a gizmo that in modern times resembles a flattened and translucent white enema-bag, but instead of water, it's filled with fiber optics, creating a thin sheet that you can lay under book pages and then light up. This instantly reveals the distinctive pattern of watermarks and chain lines that every old piece of paper possesses. And who knows? There may come a time when the physical substance of a book can as readily be traced to a manufacturer—or a region, a tree, a date of cutting—as mitochondrial DNA traces the ancestry of humans. I am being fanciful, but who knows what decades or centuries may bring? Given enough time, some fancies become facts.

Yet West is not engaged in speculation: he is all business when it comes to scholarship. That may explain why the shelves of his house eschew any showy bindings for the marked-up, old paperbacks of the classics of a working scholar. Yet as I get ready to leave for the train to Charing Cross, I can't help but blurt out a question:

"Anthony, have you ever thought of buying a Folio yourself?"

The question actually seems to surprise him.

"No," he says. "I don't collect books."

Kensal Green Cemetery, London

IT SEEMS APPROPRIATE that Kensal Green Cemetery faces a fossil shop. Along with the florists and the masons next door, it's a mute editorial on the neighborhood; just wait a million years, and we'll have human ones, too—or, at least, fossilized mums, daisies, entire shale-formation bouquets. They'll still be here. In this land of scarce real estate, where graves have regularly been ignored and built over, and where double-decker digs allow coffins to be stacked up, Kensal Green is the only cemetery in London granted a perpetual charter by Parliament. People in Britain have always recognized that graves are not for the dead, but for the living—that after a few decades and the survivors have passed along, there's not much need for the grave anymore. But Kensal Green can never be anything else. When it is full it will be left alone, and none but the gravedigger will ever develop its lands.

I trudge up to the sexton's shack. He's a burly fellow dragging on a cigarette; behind him, leaning against the shed wall, is a well-used array of picks and shovels, and a Peg-Board labeled KEYS TO THE CATACOMBS. This is where the business of dying comes alive.

"Excuse me." I lean inside. "Do you know where I could find Howard Staunton's grave?"

The sexton regards me with mild curiosity, thinks about it for a moment, then rifles through some papers.

"That's the chess bloke, innit?"

"Yes."

He draws a long, curvy line on a photocopied map, all the way to the farthest reaches of the cemetery.

"Back by the canal, 'e is."

I walk past a bristling maze of tightly packed graves; the headstones are almost atop each other. As I get farther back, the inscriptions fade; the stone turns green with lichen and orange with moss that is itself dead; the asphalt beneath my feet gives out into a muddy trail, and the weeds and the bushes grow higher and wilder. The poignant little graves set with fresh flowers in vases labeled MUM AND DAD are giving way to the forgotten dead. Amid it all is a crackled, old wooden sign jammed into the ground at a jaunty angle:

DANGER
DANGEROUS STONEWORK
& COLLAPSING GRAVES

KEEP TO THE
ROADS AND PATHWAYS

As if to prove the point, I pass an alarmingly high heap of smashed-up masonry piled up in the cold wind. But after curving along the back of the lot, I find it: a black marble headstone that bears the inscribed picture of a knight from a chess set, and a name:

HOWARD STAUNTON
1810–1874

Beneath is the inscription to his wife, Frances, and a quotation from *Henry VI*:

Oh, that I could but

—hissssss—

call these dead

—hissssss—

to life . . .

—hissssss—

It is impossible to continue, for towering over me, not fifty yards away across the canal, is an immense and rusting gasworks tank. It looks disused, but its sound says otherwise: its tubing and valvature is in incessant reptilian release.

—hisssssss—

I turn on my heel and walk past the endless expanse of muddy graves, back toward a Bakerloo-line train that will return me to Charing Cross. The cemetery has no other visitors right now, for this corner of Kensal Green is just about the loneliest spot in London. Yet in its soil is the man who brought more Folios to the world than any other in history.

Even as the Reverend Thomas Dibdin was watching London's great era of collecting come to an end along these streets by the Strand in the 1830s, Londoners could find another new obsession arising just a few buildings down from the Maggs Brothers bookshop. A hint remains at 100 Strand, above the arched doorway and grand columns of Simpson's Grand Divan, in an inlaid pattern: a checkerboard with a knight, pawns, and bishops. Today it's a stout old wood-paneled restaurant famed for its roast beef, but two centuries ago the Divan was also the birthplace of modern chess. If you were a competitive player, this was where you lived and breathed the game.

It's here that a young Howard Staunton could be seen in 1836, an unknown twenty-six-year-old making his first steps onto the board. He claimed to be the son of the Earl of Carlisle; he was said to be an Oxford dropout who had blown an inheritance of a few thousand pounds, and he had apparently done a bit of work as an actor, playing Lorenzo to Edmund Kean's Shylock. He was now in search of something with which to occupy his life, and in the Divan he could find it.

In those days it was known as the Cigar Divan, with smoke so thick in the air that passersby mistook the place for a tobacconist's shop. It might as well have been; while two great fireplaces at either end of the place kept patrons warm, their endless demand for coffee and cigars kept the Divan in business. Ordinary gentlemen gathered near the front of the Divan to read papers over their coffee, while by the fireplace in the back, chess players would begin congregating on long sofas at around noon, manning tables and issuing their traditional bet to passersby:

"Play for a shilling?"

Those that took them up usually emerged into the daylight of the Strand reeking of tobacco and rather lighter in the pocket; but Staunton watched and learned. For all the game's gentlemanly accoutrements, Staunton threw his body into chess: when he began taking the table, he astonished other players by taking hours to play games that had once been dispatched in minutes. A game with Staunton could turn into an all-day affair, stretching to twelve or thirteen hours; he combined a brilliance in his play with the simple expedient of breaking down his opponent's nerves through agonizing waits between each move. Games became almost comically psychological; one Divan match was marked by the hiring of street musicians to play cacophonously near an easily rattled player. Staunton was fond of annoying a diminutive German opponent by delaying the start of the game to make a great show of searching under the room's chairs and cushions, all the while claiming that he couldn't find him.

Only occasionally could Staunton be beaten at his own game; once, after playing for so many hours that every onlooker had drifted away, his opponent finally made a confession: "I am a poor man and cannot afford to lose this match. I must sit you out." The bluff, for once, worked on Staunton.

In fact, a great deal about Staunton's life was also a bluff. He does not appear to have actually been a child of the Earl of Carlisle; his name does not appear in any will; he does not appear on any rolls for Oxford; no record exists of him having ever performed in *The Merchant of Venice*. We do not know for sure that he was even born with the name Howard Staunton. We know scarcely a single certainty about the man, save this: by 1843, he was the world's greatest chess hustler.

Landmark chess books followed, as did a twenty-seven-year run as Britain's leading chess columnist; so did a career of playing correspondence chess games by the newly invented telegraph, and a central role in creating the world's first chess tournament for the 1851 Great Exhibition. Today the name of Staunton is synonymous with chess: the standard chess set around the world, be it a pristine array in a Moscow tournament or a battered board at a Daytona nursing home, is known as a Staunton chess set.

Yet the nerviest player the game ever produced lost his own nerve. Perhaps it was his lingering ill health after a near-fatal bout of pneumonia during a Paris match; perhaps it was simply the mellowing of age. But by the 1851 exhibition, Staunton was complaining about long matches; and when a new American player traveled from New Orleans to Britain in 1858 to challenge him, Staunton famously stalled the young man for months and finally avoided playing him altogether. His reputation never entirely recovered, and chess writers have puzzled ever since over what happened.

Curiously, to find an answer you must look not in the annals of chess but in the memoirs of an American preacher. Moncure Conway—an extraordinary Virginia protégé of Emerson's—recalled many years later a visit to Stratford-upon-Avon for a grand tercentenary Shakespeare birthday fete in 1864, where he encountered none other than Howard Staunton. Strolling through the town afterward and gushing over Staunton's chess books, the Reverend Conway was shocked to hear the grand master admit that he'd long since stopped playing chess.

Whatever for? Conway asked.

"It not only took up too much of my time," Staunton said as they went to muse over the town records of Shakespeare's family, "but I found that it demoralized players. Men have hated me and said mean things about me merely because I beat them at chess."

The game's most ruthless player, it seems, had undergone a change of heart. And, as Staunton would patiently explain, he could no longer defend his chess title for another reason. His days were now passed in the British Library—spent obsessing over a First Folio.

• • •

And here is the very Folio he held.

I pause and look back across the Rare Book Room again: hundreds of scholars are leafing through old volumes. Some may have an original owner's name scratched into the endpapers. But I may be the only one here who can name more than one of the owners, whose book has an actual traceable provenance. I'm in the hot seat again—stationed in front of a staffer—and before me is a Folio with a morocco binding that subtly fades like a sunburst finish on a guitar, from lustrous brown at its outer edge to increasing light orange and finally yellow near the spine. Centered in the front cover are a set of arms and the slightly clumsy rendering:

Rt. HONble THOs GRENVILLE

Inside there is a neatly written note in browned ink on an endpaper: *This First edition of Shakespeare is an original and perfect copy, and was purchased by me in it's first binding, and in it's original state. T.G.*

Call it the first First Folio—for Sidney Lee once did. He numbered it Folio #1. Or call it West Folio #13, or British Library shelfmark G.11631. But there is only one real name for this book, that all have given it for the last two centuries: the Grenville Folio. It is their crown jewel, a book that Dibdin once placed in his rarefied first class of Folios, that Lee later classified as 1-A quality, and which is normally displayed as the first item in the Treasures of the Library public exhibit. Today, though, it rests in my hands.

The Grenville Folio is a beautiful book. Even the faint wear tells a story, for the fading is not as severe on the back cover; presumably this Folio once sat on a shelf where it stuck farther out than other volumes, and the front of the book faced a window in Grenville's library. He hadn't kept the original binding—Grenville had it rebound not only with his own arms upon the cover, but with what is known as gauffering: that is, the outside edges of the pages are gilt, then engraved by a heated roller tool with a subtle arabesque of fanciful curlicues.

Yet it's the pages inside that have made it priceless. The book was once owned by Dr. John Monro, the head physician of Bethlem Hospital—yes, a Folio of Bedlam—and upon his death in 1792 it was snapped up by a Mr. Midgeley; when he died in 1818, Grenville grabbed it. Each generation used it lightly, and although the text has occasional tiny holes, there are no attached pages, and no telltale repairs. What is even more remarkable is that it was a good copy even when it was new. Many Folios were indifferently inked by Jaggard's assistants; yet this copy's title-page portrait is one of the few well-inked original portraits I've seen. The effect is startling. Droeshout's artistry—right down to the stubble on Bill's chin—only becomes apparent when you have a properly inked copy. And very, very few people do.

That is why, even as Howard Staunton dodged his chess rivals, he held this book and contemplated a move greater than any he had made on a checkerboard: to photograph its pages and make endless copies available to the world outside the library's walls.

Faux Folios had existed for years already; after George Steevens's complaint in 1793 of textual Frankensteins sewn together from bashed-up volumes, it was the next logical step, in 1807, for Westminster printers Edward and Joseph Wright to re-create an entire First Folio from scratch. With the invention of photography decades away, re-creating a Folio meant setting type for an entire book by hand, painstakingly matching the pagination and line breaks, and engraving a whole new look-alike title-page portrait. The result was remarkable, not least because authenticity was still fairly easy to achieve. Printing in 1807 was not so different from in Jaggard's time, after all; neither wood-pulp paper nor rotary presses had been invented yet. Mass production of books was decades away, and a printer from Jaggard's shop could have walked into the Wright shop on Denmark Court and still felt more or less at home.

It helped that their editor was Francis Douce, the keeper of manuscripts at the British Museum and a daily stop back when Steevens made the morning rounds of London. In Douce's capable hands, the 1807 facsimile became almost *too* convincing. Aside from a single easily removed note, to the untrained eye it looks like the real thing; the only way to readily discern the two is by the watermark in the paper. The title page was a particularly masterful copy, and the edition was soon prized by dealers, who raided it to replace missing title pages from original Folios. To this day, well-intentioned "First Folio" leads often have an 1807 folio at the end of them.

For the less well-intentioned, not much stops the creation of modern fakes. I once chatted with a Manhattan dealer who revealed to me how he'd come up with a replacement title page without cutting into the 1807 Wright on his shelf.

"We had to create a facsimile title page for a client with a Folio." He shook his head. "A scary experience."

"How come?"

"What we did was—well—we just took some old paper, got a good scan of Droeshout off the Web, and ran the paper through a laser printer."

"That's it?"

"That's it. It looked so good—*you couldn't tell.* It's frightening. We're upfront about what is a facsimile and what isn't, but as for whoever the next owner is, well . . ." He let his point hang in the air.

I understood why he didn't want to cut into his Wright folio: they've become rare themselves. It was a short-lived venture, after all. Within months of releasing his folio, John Wright caught pneumonia on a hunting trip and died. His brother and partner Joseph Wright took over, and about a year later he also died. Then their third brother, Edward Wright, stepped in, and a year later *he* died. Any survivors left from the project might well have run for their lives.

In the decades that followed, the best source for mock-Folio pages instead proved to be an extraordinary fellow named John Harris. A protégé of Fuseli's and a Royal Academy–trained artist, he began working for the British Library in 1820 as perhaps the greatest restoration artist the country ever produced. Armed with nothing more than a pen and ink, he specialized at re-creating by hand everything from missing letters to entire missing pages from old manuscripts. He became so good at it that years after one of his retouching projects, British Library staff were puzzled over which part of a book was original and which part re-created. They finally called in Harris, who after closely inspecting the pages admitted that *he* was stumped.

"It was only after some considerable search," a staffer later recalled drily, "that the artist was able to detect his own handiwork."

In re-creating the Droeshout portrait, Harris was not just good— he almost was better than Droeshout himself. The New York Public Library owns a Folio that, in a pure spirit of perversity, a previous owner has bound in not one, not two, but *three* title pages. One is a Harris, and the other two are 1623 originals. Try as you will to look back and forth between the pages, *you cannot tell* which ones are real and which is not.

Harris never found an equal. One more try at a facsimile was made in 1864 by London bookseller Lionel Booth; it was painstakingly edited but effected what he termed a more "cheerful semblance" by employing modern type. The result was all right, yet somehow all wrong. It quickly wound up in the remainder pile. No real substitute existed for the old-fashioned craft of John Wright or the obsessive artistry of John Harris; the world would simply have to wait for a whole new way to magically re-create a Folio.

And that's just what it got.

"Here." The clerk hands me the folio and then turns away. They're unconcerned now—it's just a copy, after all, as the title page itself informs me:

Shakespeare

the

First Folio Edition of 1623

Reproduced Under the Immediate Supervision of

HOWARD STAUNTON

From the Originals in the Libraries of

Bridgewater House and the British Museum

by PHOTO-LITHOGRAPHY

Yes, just a copy. But the library's date stamp of *13 FE 66* tells a different story: it is the *first* photographic copy ever made of an entire published work.

Today we blithely buy new facsimiles of old books or google up their scans on our screens; but here, at the dawn of photography, Staunton had done something amazing. There were, as of 1866, still only thirty-nine or so known First Folios. Those with ready access to a Folio were probably to be numbered only in the hundreds; you could spend your entire life studying Shakespeare and still go to your grave without ever having laid eyes on a First Folio.

And so this book that I am holding is miraculous; through it, the Folio became immortal.

"By the aid of this unerring agent," Staunton hails to the reader, ". . . [we] obtain imperishable copies of any manuscript and printed book, so closely resembling the original as to defy discrimination."

I settle in to turn the pages; the immense project was gradually issued in sixteen affordable parts, which bought time for Staunton and his assistants to work with the newfangled photo-printing facilities at the Ordnance Survey Department in Southampton, where delicate photographic plates were coated with transfer ink and pressed onto lithos for etching. The process had not quite been perfected yet: the lettering is curiously grainy, as if printed with a mix of ink and sand. By the bottom of page 41 in the *Merry Wives of Windsor*, the type and borders threaten to dematerialize altogether. Yet to a reader of Shakespeare in 1866, this book was a revelation: for the first time, the original text of Shakespeare, unmediated, had come to everyone. What was more, the Folio could never be lost again—not to fires, not to scribbling children, not to sinking ships.

"There is no deed in the history of Shakespeare literature which deserves more thanks . . ." proclaimed one of Staunton's fellow scholars. "To his indefatigable and persistent exertions is it mainly due that Shakespeare is delivered from one source of destruction."

Perhaps it's not so surprising that Staunton largely gave up a chess career to become the man who saved Shakespeare. When he married in 1849, he quietly entered his father's name on the certificate as William Staunton. It was hardly a document he'd have expected to be made public. But William Staunton was landed gentry in Warwickshire and had died just the year before; perhaps Howard, never formally acknowledged as a legitimate son, could only now dare to reveal his parentage. If he could not claim legitimacy from his father, he inherited his passions: for the elder Staunton was one of the country's great antiquarian collectors—a rival of previous facsimilist Francis Douce, in fact—and he'd proudly possessed Shakespearian documents dating back to the days when a Staunton had been the godparent to the bard's son.

If Howard could not loudly proclaim his parentage, he could at least be a friend to Shakespeare's progeny once again.

His book, with a presence so seemingly unremarkable in the piles on my library desk, was more important than Staunton could ever know. Writing on chess and Shakespeare until the very end, in 1874 he collapsed of a heart attack at his writing desk in Kensington and passed on to his reward. But his book lived on, growing in wild profusion. Two years after his death, the London firm of Chatto and Windus reissued his facsimile; a decade later, they sold the well-worn plates to America, where Funk and Wagnalls issued a cheap edition in 1887, from which identical descendants still remain in print—each a little more frayed and unreliable, yet each wondrously multiplying Staunton's labors. What began with this library's gilt Folio has now gone through student knapsacks and scholars' desks, and through distant library shelves to the reach of untold millions. And one of those cheap new copies of Staunton—that living image of this city's finest Folios—came into the hands of a young man in Brooklyn named Henry Clay Folger.

ACT IV

East Capitol Street, Washington, D.C.

IF GEOGRAPHY IS any indication, then the Folger Library is the fourth branch of American government. It sits, after all, across the lawn from the Capitol and down the block from the Supreme Court. Yet that's not the first thing you notice as you walk up East Capitol Street; what you notice are the houses. A few old brick houses have been preserved here, and they remain very much inhabited. There's something charming in the notion of living in a house where your first step outside in the morning has the Supreme Court porticoes looming over your head, or where you can nonchalantly start mowing your lawn while networks frantically set up their cameras on the steps across the street. You'll never know this from news coverage: they always have their cameras facing the Court steps. Yet on this block, amid the awesome crush of history, the unawed living maintain a stubborn tenancy.

I walk inside the cool, underlit atrium of the Folger. A folio is always on display here; I watch at least three visitors miss it altogether. Past an inner sanctum of an admittance desk, though, an arched doorway opens into another realm altogether: out there may be the Folger, but in here is the Library. Its appearance has not changed since *National Geographic* sent a photographer by in 1951. A grand stained-glass window still radiates over a long expanse of thick wooden tables and stout chairs: it's Edwardian collegiate across the horizontal, but a dizzying Elizabethan great hall along the vertical plane. The floor still has the same spongy green carpet that makes you want to either tackle a Milton scholar or throw a long bomb down the forty yards to the reference desk. But you can't do these things, alas; at the far end of the library, a painted wooden bust of Shakespeare maintains a sober watch over the proceedings. He's flanked on either side by oil paintings, and in one of them I meet another man's gaze: Henry Clay Folger.

The son of a struggling Brooklyn hatmaker, Folger was a scholarship kid who drew the son of an oilman, Charles Pratt, as his roommate at Amherst. Folger's habit of finding solace in Shakespeare's plays deep into the night didn't annoy his roommate too much, which was fortunate—because when the hatmaking business went bust, the Pratt family paid Folger's way, then in 1879 gave him his first job after college. The oil business saved Henry Folger; but what it saved him for was, in his few spare moments, the study of Shakespeare. When he got married, he gave to his new bride an American reprint of Staunton's Folio facsimile. "Here you may see Shakespeare's plays as they were actually given to the world," he told her earnestly.

And indeed she *could* see them—because the edition cost all of $1.25.

Folger was not always fated to remain a Pratt Oil clerk. He rose up in the organization, then, when it was acquired, shot upward through the ranks of Standard Oil. By 1911, he was one of its highest-ranking executives—which, considering that its chairman, John D. Rockefeller, had become the world's wealthiest man, hints at why

Folger had long stopped needing to buy facsimiles. He was buying the real thing now.

And he was buying *lots* of them.

After straining to buy a Fourth Folio for $107 at a New York auction in 1889—he was still so strapped that he needed a month afterward to pull the money together to pay for it—Folger rose to acquire more pay and more books. Working for the country's most ruthless monopoly hardened him into a savvy negotiator: he operated on the sly, quietly buying up Folios from auctions, then—after Sidney Lee published his 1902 Folio census—using the census like a sales catalog, targeting one owner after the next and offering them money. The ones he couldn't convince, he offered more money—and then, if they balked, even more money. If that didn't work, more telegrams to dealers and shrewdly timed raises in bidding followed—for years.

"Henry," Rockefeller once chided him while they were out golfing, "I see from the papers that you just paid $100,000 for a book!"

"Now, John," Folger demurred, "you know better than anybody else how the newspapers exaggerate . . . If you buy something for $10,000, it becomes $100,000 in print."

Folger remained secretive even with his boss about how much he was buying, and indeed that he was buying at all. When the New York Public Library mounted a major Shakespeare exhibit in 1916, they tartly noted that Folger was the only collector in America who refused to loan them anything. This might have been bad press, but to Folger it was just good business: he did not want anyone to know what he owned. "I have persistently avoided all publicity," he would explain, "feeling that book-buying would be done more cheaply and successfully if there was no advertising."

The extent of Folger's determination at acquiring any and all

Shakespeariana might have defied belief anyway. When, utterly inexplicably, a previously unseen 1594 quarto of *Titus Andronicus* turned up in the hut of a Swedish peasant, of all the world's collectors it was Folger who swiftly cabled a London dealer and sent a courier to Sweden. A few days and £2,000 later, Folger was—and remains—the owner of the world's only original edition of *Titus Andronicus*.

In fact, a great many books were Folger's. After spending nine years secretly buying houses along this street, Folger oversaw the groundbreaking of his future library in 1930. He never saw more than shovels in the dirt: two weeks later, he died of a heart attack. Only when he was gone did the size of his collection become apparent. Early on, Stratford's head librarian had been amazed to hear rumors that Folger had acquired five Folios, not knowing that by that point Folger actually owned fifty. By the time Folger died, the man some had fancifully dubbed Forty Folio Folger had, in fact, *seventy-nine* Folios.

He had half of the world's known copies.

That was the least of it: the executors discovered that Folger had accumulated a staggering two hundred thousand more books, paintings, and manuscripts, packed into 2,019 wooden crates in warehouses in Brooklyn and Manhattan. He was, in short, a return to the great book maniacs of the 1820s—what mills and sea power had once created in the Old World, oil and railways had conjured again in the New. But unlike the collectors of old, Folger had determined that his collection would stay together after he died.

What started it all wasn't an actual Folio, but that worn-out reprint of Howard Staunton. They still have it here, and it's perhaps the cheapest and most common book in the Folger's holdings. But, his wife would later muse, it was the cornerstone of this entire library.

· · ·

I've seen the cornerstone; now I want the columns that hold everything up.

"How about Folio One?" I keep asking Betsy, the Reading Room's supervisor.

"Well..."

Folio #1 is *the* one; you might as well ask Fort Knox to hand over its gold. Granted, the Folger's friendlier than it used to be; in its early years, it was perhaps the world's only library with armed guards. Even so, I still need a good reason to look at the Folios— and a good letter of introduction—and given the boggling array of seventy-nine Folios to choose from, a good idea of which Folio to request. "Which Folio?" is a question that can only be asked at perhaps a half dozen libraries in the world, but here it takes on a vertiginous quality.

But if I can't have their best Folio, then—

"I'd like," I announce, "your *worst* Folio."

"Our... worst Folio?"

And their worst, I have decided, is probably Folio #66. When it arrives, Betsy does a double take. "What *happened* to this one?" she wonders as she hands it over to me.

Indeed.

Number 66 is thin—like a Folio after a crash diet—or as if a Folio had been shaved down with a carpenter's plane. Its edges appear to have been chewed by mice, and its marbled paper cover is flaking off a nearly unmarked binding; nothing on it indicates that it is anything other than an old accounting ledger, save for the fading, crudely inked words half-hidden in the cover: FIRST FOLIO, 1623.

It's a first, all right—namely, the first one I've seen that didn't even have at least a cheap copy of a title page inserted. There's no title page at all; what it does have, though, is a dent running through the entire length of the book on the bottom right corner, as if it had been used to prop up a table leg—which, I'm beginning to suspect, it probably was. In fact, when the London book dealer Sotheran bought this in 1907, the firm paid a mere £45—about what a good Folio fetched in 1790. It was sold more or less at cost to Folger and mailed with an ignominious note that it was "sold not subject to return." When you page through it today, you can see why. Virtually every page has little tears, and some have frighteningly large ones; when I get to page 17 of *The Tempest*, I find the entire bottom third of the page raggedly torn away—just *gone*.

> *This fellow not drowne: Now blasphemy*
> *Grace ore-bord, not an oath on shore,*
> *nd?*

There's more: *Two Gentlemen of Verona* has what appears to be a sprinkling of soot in its gutter; *Measure for Measure* has a smear of glue across page 84; *Henry VI* got splatted with strawberry jam. The latter's page 161 has been torn away so violently that a triangle of remaining paper sticks up like a tail fin between pages 160 and 163. The Folio ends altogether at *Henry VIII*: this Folio has no tragedies, only comedy and history.

It's all rather shocking: I've become so used to seeing repairs or replacement leaves, no matter how clumsily added, that to find a Folio in its raw state is a revelation. This is what restorers and book dealers used to find in barns and attics two centuries ago. This is how Folios once were; and when you see something like this, you can understand why the old dealers so readily cannibalized Folios to make new ones. What else were they going to do? Just leave them like . . . *this*?

Along with the text, the context seems largely lost, too: the endpapers show a pen inscription of GEORGE GWINN, written in a hand that would date it to about 1675. There's never been attribution of the name, but I see that back then a George Gwynn served as MP for Radnor. The crown's records show that he pulled down a £1,000 annual income, the sort of money that could buy a fine library. Gwynn also served as the sheriff of Monmouth—and if he could only see what later owners did to his book, I imagine he'd have them arrested.

Folio #66 is what you get when the past has left you with barely anything; but what happens when you get a Folio that still has *everything*?

"Could I see Folio forty-two?" I ask.

"Forty-two," Betsy says, and the request whisks into the depths of the building.

When the book arrives, I see a nearby scholar lean over a little to look. Although Folios are the crown jewels of the Folger, the oilman's acquisitions were so vast that most visiting scholars are not Shakespeareans. Yet the thing is clearly arresting: *it's in the original binding.* Not an almost-original like Dr. Williams's copy at Sotheby's; not a battered eighteenth-century binding like Sam Johnson's, nor a splendid gold-engraved Regency number like Lord Grenville's—no, this one is the real thick calf binding, brown and plain as a polished block of wood, and with barely any adornment save for some faint floral stamps in the corners.

And what's more—and nearly as rare—it still has every single one of its original pages. The title page is almost comically homely: about a quarter has been roughly torn away in a triangle at the top right-hand side; somebody laid in a repair sheet and crudely wrote in half of the missing title words . . . and, for good measure, filled in some wisps of hair from the top of Shakespeare's head. It looks like a repair a Jacobean child was sentenced to perform for tearing Daddy's book. Just to complete the effect, hints of paper are torn away from right over the bard's face; apparently someone once pasted a label over poor Will's mug.

Yet it is lovely to me. What makes #42 among the loveliest of Folios is its endpapers. In the front are two inscriptions that look to be from the seventeenth century—Henery Prudence, a Norfolk name dating to that time, and a "Robert Toomson of Stocksbey in the County of Norfolke"—that would be Stokesby, where Thomson remains a common name. At the back, an eighteenth-century hand has practiced penmanship exercises with individual letters, done some quick column addition to 928—though 928 of what, we shall never know—and then proclaimed:

John Elden
his Book
1714

Go to the front, and you are confronted with this inscription: *This Book is my Aunt's Elden's of Systrand to be sent to Mr. Benj. Elden a dyer in St Michael's of Colney, Norwich.* Nearby an old price is written in: *£1 10 d.*

Nobody has sussed out these owners before, but I can make a fair guess. The wonder of Folio #42 is that by some offhand inscriptions, you can trace an astonishing amount of history. Take John Elden: dig around Norwich history a bit, and you'll find him listed as newly deceased in a 1728 land-transfer document. One of his sons receiving property is . . . Benjamin Elden. Dig further, and you'll find Benjamin was something of a book collector; Benjamin Elden of Norwich is listed on the subscriber list to James Foster's 1749 *Discourses on All the Principal Branches of Natural Religion*. Dig further still, and you'll find a heraldic inscription on the wall of Octagon chapel: Benjamin Elden died on June 17, 1762, at the age of sixty-two. If that seems rather grand for a dyer, it's because he was likely a *doctor* of St. Michael's—which was the chapel in Colney.

So where did it go from there?

Look back at the front preliminaries: here's a bit of browned ink: *J. Brooke ex dono prodicti Dni B. Elden.*

Not very promising. "J." Brooke? Not even a full name or a date? Ah, but you don't need it. Benjamin Elden's home village of Colney has the virtue of modesty: it has scarcely ever exceeded more than a hundred inhabitants. Look there around the time that Elden died, and you discover a John Brooke—an Anglican minister, and precisely the sort of fellow who'd write inscriptions in Latin, and who would acquire books from a subscriber to *Principal Branches of Natural Religion*.

And what of Brooke? *He* married Frances Moore, the daughter of another Norfolk clergyman. Frances made a name for herself by going to London and anonymously publishing a newspaper in 1755 called *The Old Maid*. It included nods to her good friend Samuel Johnson—a fellow Folio owner—and she quarreled a bit with still another Folio owner, David Garrick. Her husband eventually became a military chaplain in Canada, where they were garrisoned near their friend Robert Cholmondeley—who also owned a Folio—and there she secured her fame by becoming Canada's first novelist. Back in England, she became a playwright and went on to run the Haymaket Opera. It was about then that Fanny Burney described her as "very short and fat, and squint; but she has the art of showing agree-able ugliness." And Fanny, of course, was the *sister* of Charles Burney Jr., *another* Folio owner.

We can go further.

Frances and her husband, John, retired to Sleaford, Lincolnshire, where they died within a few days of each other in 1789—one shud-ders to think of what was going about back then that could bump off two old worthies so quickly. The book then resurfaces with a book-plate. The Folger notes that there was once a bookplate for the Grimston family, yet I see none now, which—ah!—would account for that old glue still stuck to the portrait's face. And who were these glue-happy Grimstons? Most likely the Grimstons of Grimston Hall—in, naturally, the village of Grimston Garth—an ancient clan some eighty miles north of where the Brooke family expired. One of the clan, Florence Grimston, had attempted to write a romance her-self as a youth, and I suppose a Folio would be a fine family heirloom for an authoress. But, alas, neither she nor her work could last; and in 1916, a London dealer wrote to Folger of "a quite recently discovered copy," unlisted in any census, "found . . . in an old house in Yorkshire (owned by the same family for 400 years or so we understand)." Fol-ger offered to have it shipped over himself by the SS *St. Louis*, "in-cluding Insurance against War risks"—this is 1916, after all—and wired over £1,250 for a volume that still bears a one-pound price in-side its cover.

Which reminds me.

"Any word on Folio number one?" I ask Betsy hopefully.

"Hmm," she explains.

What, exactly, are they *doing* with all those Folios back there?

Folger Shakespeare Library, Washington, D.C.

IT'S NOT FOLIO #1, but one of the Folger's great treasures is invisible to the visiting scholar: you can stand just a few feet away at the book request desk and never even know it.

"So it's in here." Georgianna ushers me through a door. She's a Shakespeare scholar and the Folger's reference head; yet in the middle of her grand and capacious library, we are suddenly alone and confined in a room full of toner cartridges. She nods toward the recess of the room.

"That's the one?"

"That's the one."

Shoved between a stepladder and shelves of discarded PC keyboards, there sits a boxy and hulking contraption. Nearly as tall as a man and bristling with black knobs, cold steel toggle switches, and polished optical gear: a device from the Vaguely Sinister era of sheet-metal construction.

"We don't really use it these days," she half apologizes.

But people did—once. A pile of old seat cushions are unceremoniously stowed atop the unit, but over the row of toggle switches a simple black plaque remains visible:

Manufactured & Sold by
Mico Engineering Company
Bladensburg, Maryland
Model L, Serial No. L1047

I run my finger over the two other words engraved upon it: HIN-
MAN COLLATOR.

Modern textual scholarship began with bombs—or, at least, with a
problem that those bombs presented. For while it's one thing for
warplanes to hit a target, it's quite another to measure the damage
they inflict. So, after Shakespeare scholar Charlton Hinman joined
the U.S. Navy as a cryptographer in 1941, he heard of an intriguing
idea being considered by military intelligence. What if you ran before and after aerial reconnaissance photos in quick succession, creating a primitive motion picture? Any change between "before" and
"after" would be interpreted by the brain as movement, with bombed
gun emplacements rather appropriately appearing to shake violently.
But an intractable problem arose: how could you take before and after photos from precisely the same spot in the sky?

The idea of running two similar but subtly different pictures in
quick succession to look for telltale flickers of change was not an entirely new notion. In 1904 the German instrument-maker Carl Pulf-
rich invented the "blink comparator," which flickered images fast
enough for astronomers to spot changes in photographic plates
taken on different nights. Subtle differences—a passing comet, say—
cause a telltale wobble in the image. The blink comparator helped
astronomer Clyde Tombaugh discover Pluto in 1930, and the same
concept—brought to a scholar's attention by that abortive wartime

attempt to use it for military intelligence—would eventually revolutionize a very earthbound task: literary scholarship.

As a doctoral student studying Shakespeare at the University of Virginia, Hinman had pored over early editions of Shakespeare determined to pin down "what Shakespeare actually wrote." Easier said than done: no two books have exactly the same combination of corrected and uncorrected pages, so that a riot of variations make it nearly impossible to determine what the "real" text is. In one Folio, Laertes yells out at Ophelia's graveside, "O treble woe . . ." But in another Folio he says, "Oh, terrible woer." For centuries, the only way to untangle these texts was manual collation, to go back and forth from one copy to another to check each word and punctuation mark. It's an agonizingly slow process dubbed the Wimbledon Method for its endless back-and-forth head-twisting. Hinman's prewar doctoral project of manually collating and analyzing multiple copies of *Othello* took him years.

What then about collating all of Shakespeare's plays? Though the immense collection gathered here at the Folger presented an extraordinary opportunity, Hinman estimated the task would take at least forty years. But what if, he wondered, the concept of a blink comparator was modified? What if what you were comparing were not planets or bombing runs, but . . . books?

Georgianna switches the unit on and it starts up with a whir. It resembles a chem lab table with a ventilation hood, but the earliest prototypes were rather less professional-looking. An inveterate tinkerer, Hinman set about cannibalizing parts for his project and mused later that he'd procured "a pair of ordinary microfilm projectors (scavenged from the Navy), some pieces of a wooden apple box (abstracted from a trash pile), some heavy cardboard (begged from the Folger bindery), and parts of a rusty Erector set (more or less hijacked from the small son of a close personal friend)." Add mirrors and an eyepiece, and he was ready to succeed where military intelligence had failed.

There was just one problem: it didn't work.

Hinman wasn't actually comparing books: he had built his prototype to compare the microfilms of books. Microfilm's prone to smudges, scratches, and blurring, so Hinman's blinking motion picture was bedeviled by phantom shakes. The only way to avoid the problem was by using the priceless old books themselves. By 1949, Hinman had completely redesigned his machine. The new model was the 450-pound sheet-metal beast that glowers before me now. This Hinman includes a system of blinking lamps and mirrors arranged around books on two folio-size, velvet-covered wooden racks. Screw adjustments and lenses are everywhere for aligning and focusing the two books—the thing's like a mule bred of a workbench and an optician's lens tester—but it's never been a perfect arrangement.

"These can be hard on the books," Georgianna admits. "The bulbs get quite hot."

Even so, libraries around the world eagerly bought Hinman Collators from Hinman and his builder, Arthur Johnson. At prices that eventually reached $11,000 a pop, a Hinman was no small investment, but the results were dramatic. Hinman himself crunched a lifetime's worth of collating First Folios into just nineteen months. Other scholars, collating everything from Nathaniel Hawthorne's *Scarlet Letter* to Mark Twain's *Tom Sawyer*, published a flood of newly definitive editions of classic literary works. By the 1970s many major universities had a Hinman Collator, as did the British Museum and the Library of Congress.

Even the CIA allegedly bought one of these—though they wouldn't say what for.

"What you're looking at here," Georgianna says as she lays out the pages on the collator racks and carefully adjusts them, "is from *Two Gentlemen of Verona.*"

I nod and glance at them over her shoulder. They're from Folios #34 and #68 in the Folger collection—the first previously belonged to a Victorian watercolorist, and the other to a distant cousin of P. G. Wodehouse's—and she's chosen the same page of act 3, scene 1, from their respective copies. From a few feet away the texts look identical.

"You put your eyes up to here," she indicates a binocular eyepiece.

My forehead presses into a red piece of felt over the eyepiece, and my eyes take a moment to focus. What appears in the viewfinder seems to be a single page—one that exists only in my brain, as it is the optical marriage of the two texts before me.

"Okay."

"You can have both blinking, or one side or the other steadily lit as the other blinks," she explains as she flicks a switch. "We'll try blinking the left side first."

Twitch twitch twitch.

It's curiously disorienting. Experienced users, viewing pages as a whole image rather than reading the words on them, will run their eyes in an S-pattern down the page in seconds—much faster than they could read the actual text. I try to stop reading the words and instead read the picture, and a flickering and nearly subliminal phantom text flickers just within the edge of my perception.

"Wait . . ."

"Do you see it?"

"I . . ."

mine, twice or thrice in
(blink)(blink)
mine twice, or thrice in

"The comma! They moved the comma!"

"Mmm-hmm. Let's set both to blink."

Tick tick tick go the lights—and from under the door of our supply closet it must look like there's a lightning storm inside. Through the lenses the pages take the appearance of a cheap hypno-effect in an old horror flick—yet the effect on the text variants is even more dramatic. Just a few words later in the same line I see:

mine, twice or thrice in that last Article
(blinkblinkblinkblink)
mine twice, or thrice in that Article

"*Last,*" I mutter as Shakespeare's missing text flickers up into my brain. "It's *last.*"

"It is," she says.

Collators like the Folger's are becoming a rare sight: fifty-eight are known to have been built, and I suspect the number of unscrapped survivors might be counted on your fingers. It's tempting to assume, as with so many other mechanical-optical gizmos of the past, that computers have supplanted them—for indeed such programs are being hacked at by text editors—but the accuracy isn't quite there yet. When you're looking to find missing commas and infinitesimal spelling variants in Renaissance typesets, programs that still can't even read modern fonts perfectly just aren't going to cut it.

Curiously, researchers have gone *lower* tech: the Hinmans have been supplanted not by computers but by mirrors. Instead of relying on the perception of motion, newer, portable "optical collators" use the same stereoscopic principle as a child's View-Master. The brain naturally takes two separate images—one from each eye—and combines them to create a perception of depth. By lining up mirrors and positioning your head just so, you can train your left eye on one book, your right eye on another; variations in the merged image appear to float off the page.

"It's a strange sensation," admits Carter Hailey. At first glance he's just another researcher out in the Folger Reading Room with a briefcase—but his contains something more than the usual sheaves of notes and tin of Altoids. He's the inventor of the collator's latest and simplest refinement into a two-mirror system—a setup so simple that it fits into a briefcase. He first invented it a decade ago, when he needed to collate *Piers Plowman*.

"This is a fairly nice version I've got here," he says as he adjusts his gear onto the Reading Room desk, an old quarto at his side of *Pierce Pennilesse, His Supplication to the Divell*. "But, you know, you could build one of these out of mirrors and drafting-lamp swing-arms."

I watch in disbelief, then look back over to the supply room, where I've just operated a competing machine that was nearly the cost of a Buick.

"So I could build one of these for thirty bucks?"

"More or less."

It takes a while to adjust it to perfection—the mirrors have to be just so—but the elegance and simplicity is so startling that it's almost inconceivable that this is what's replaced the Hinman.

"Now here's a neat thing you can't do with the Hinman." He clicks open his laptop. "Watch this."

He taps into EEBO—or Early English Books Online, an

immense scanned database. EEBO contains 100,000 of the 125,000 known titles published in English through 1700, the latest migratory wave of old books into imaging technology. Rather like the Hinman, its roots extend back to World War II: while mechanical collation grew from bombing raids, back in England librarians were frantically microfilming their books to preserve them from the other side's V-1s. Now, with scanning, whole libraries exist in an invulnerable ether.

The scanned image of a play pops up: it's another copy of *Pierce Pennilesse.*

"Now if we set this up correctly," Carter says, "then you can collate the online scan against the printed copy we have here."

This takes a moment to sink in.

"You mean I'm using the screen as one of my books? Isn't there distortion? One of these is 3-D, and the other is a flat screen."

When you have one eye on each, he points out, they're *both* flat. The depth is created in your head with both eyes working together.

"So . . . wait. If you could tap into two separate scanned copies, could you do this with two laptops?"

"Sure."

"So I could be in Antarctica and collate one copy from Japan and another one from here?"

"Well"—he pauses—"yes, you could."

The thought is overwhelming: you can take two books that you've never held, that maybe don't even exist anymore—as long as a scan was made of them first—and create in your head a phantasmal third book.

"That," I conclude, "is nuts."

"It's optics," he says. "Go on and give it a try."

I put my head in position with the mirror and wait for the two images to resolve into one. Though the Hinman is a bit disorienting, it's surefire in its operation: you press your face up to the eyepiece and wait for the subtle movie to start. But Hailey's collator has an element of magic to it: your head and eyes must be just right, and then a previously invisible depth forms in your head. It's all rather like the old Magic Eye pictures; but instead of looking for a picture of a unicorn inside a rosebush, I'm looking for hidden meaning in a thicket of text.

"The text becomes topographic in nature," he explains as I wait for my eyes to adjust. Even pages that have been reset with identical text but slight variations in spacing—a difference invisible to the naked eye—become immediately apparent. "The whole page leaps up in a jumble," Carter adds.

I stare for a while, unable to quite focus, not seeing it, not getting it—the unicorn is not leaping out to me—until . . . until . . . *It does.*

"I'll be damned," I breathe.

Hinman himself never saw his invention gathering dust; he died in 1977. Though he and his partner, Arthur Johnson, had even tried hawking collators to banks to detect forgeries, and to pharmaceutical companies to catch misprinted labels, neither of them ever saw much money from their machines. Theirs was a labor of love, subsidized in part by a more profitable invention of Johnson's, the Targeteer: a poor man's clay-pigeon thrower that tossed beer cans into the air for soused gun-owners to blast away at. It's all a long way from discovering planets and analyzing bombing runs—but then again, it wouldn't be the first time that a few beers have helped coax out an old writer's secrets.

The point of a Targeteer, at least, is easy enough to understand.

But once you find the textual variants with a Hinman or a Hailey collator ... what exactly does that mean? After taking on the project of collating this library's Folios, Hinman himself discovered that, well, he wasn't exactly finding anything meaningful. When he published his results in 1963 they revealed the occasional word restored here and there on each page. But what exactly did it add up to?

By his count, Hinman found "just over five hundred" variants in 898 pages; however, examining it closely, folio scholar Peter Blayney later noted that a hundred of those were due to bad inking—they weren't real variants at all—and that nearly all of the rest were easily dismissed typos or broken bits of type that a reader could still interpret the intended meaning of. In fact, of substantive variants that change the meaning of the line, Hinman only found three in the entire Folio. It gets worse: other Shakespeare scholars in the past had already caught two of those. So that leaves . . .

One.

Imagine if years of work—countless hours spent tinkering with apple crates and Erector sets and lenses—endless days scrupulously lining up pairs of Folios and sitting in a room with flashes of lightning and headaches—imagine if that netted you this:

> **Aemilia**
> *Alas (Iago) my Lord hath so bewhor'd her,*
> *Throwne such dispight, and heavy termes upon her*
> *That true hearts cannot bear it.*
>
> (*Othello, IV, ii*)

The variant, in that final line, was *heart*—so it is Desdemona who is unable to bear it, rather than Aemilia and other witnesses. That one word—that one letter—is the only real variant that Hinman personally discovered.

True hearts cannot bear it, indeed.

With years of work seemingly gone for naught, Hinman made two extraordinary leaps. The first was parlaying his intimate knowledge and access to Folger Folios into a beautiful new full-size facsimile edition for W. W. Norton—a "dream Folio" that cherry-picked the best pages from twenty-nine different copies. To this day, it remains the standard facsimile for scholars. His other great leap, though, was to stop focusing on the literal meaning of the Folio wording and instead use seemingly trivial variants to pursue the *people* behind it.

Most of us habitually make the same typos over and over—F. Scott Fitzgerald, for instance, was always setting his characters off to sail in a "yatch." By tracing the same errors and idiosyncratic spellings through the Folio, though, Hinman brilliantly traced and identified the compositors in Jaggard's shop who'd set each page. Multiple men set type for any given book, but until now nobody had known how many had set the type for the Folio. But Hinman knew: five.

Most of the Folio was set by two experienced compositors, known today only as Compositors A and B. Two others, the equally mysterious C and D, show up to set a number of the comedies. But upon the fifth, the heavy hand of history has fallen: Compositor E. This compositor set all of *Romeo and Juliet*, *Titus Andronicus*, and half of *King Lear*—and was miserable at it. Is France "hot-blooded" or "hot-bloodied"? Do "Rats oft bite the holy cords a twaine" . . . or do they bite *holly* cords? Best not ask Compositor E, because he muffed both lines in *Lear*.

"Compositor E . . . was evidently expected to make many errors. Nor," Hinman notes, "did he disappoint them."

But why was E expected to make mistakes? Since Hinman knew who was apprenticing for Jaggard at the time, he could pinpoint the culprit: a hapless seventeen-year-old from Hampshire named John Leason. Over the years successive scholars have edged the total count of likely compositors up to eight—adding Compositors F, G, and H. But Leason remains the same butterfingered E. His comically bad luck was to have Jaggard hand him the worst teen job imaginable: imagine if your crummy high school shifts at McDonald's were still getting pored over by scholars four centuries from now. What's more, imagine if your handiwork was kept in a subterranean vault, preserved until the end of time.

Actually, that last part isn't so fanciful at all.

SCENE iii.

Level C, Folger Shakespeare Library

I'VE BEEN BOTHERING her for days: Can I see it? Can I see it? Betsy walks in, sporting a purple outfit and taking her mark, as if we're preparing for a stage performance. I ask for Folio #1: they tell me the person in charge isn't here today, come back tomorrow, we have to check with preservation, et cetera; players then exit stage left.

"About Folio One," I start.

"Yes," she says. "It'll be here in twenty minutes."

I'm stunned.

"Oh," I manage.

Twenty minutes, it turns out, feels like an extraordinarily long time when you're standing in a quiet reading room. After a few minutes, I can take it no more.

"I'll be right back," I promise Betsy. "I'm off for tea."

It's where everyone else is headed anyway. Each day, from 3:00 to 3:30, a steady stream of scholars, librarians, guards, and staff make their way down a couple of flights of stairs, past a pile of haphazardly stacked chairs, and follow the sound of muted voices into a subterranean, fluorescent-lit room. A break room, in any other setting; but here, it's teatime, and a daily Folger ritual.

The whole gang's here: the Milton scholars, the staffers, the Baconians. Someone is talking about an MLA panel at one table; his tablemate is fretting about getting her Subaru's gearbox fixed. Much in the way that camping makes a can of baked beans the best thing you have ever tasted, reading four-hundred-year-old books all day without a break makes a cup of tea the best thing you've ever drunk. After savoring mine, I start leafing through my files on Folio #1.

The first letter, dating from 1899 and signed by bookseller A. B. Railton, describes how he'd been cataloging and "weeding out worthless books" from the library of one Conigsby Sibthorp, in the family seat of Canwick Hall in Lincolnshire. Childless and often absorbed in schemes to modernize his village, Conigsby was the son of an eccentric local MP known primarily for his hatred of newfangled railroads. The Sibthorps seem to have had little interest in the old books that had been lying about their ancestral abode; in fact, they'd set up a billiards room in their library. After finishing with Sibthorp's library, Railton was led by a servant to an outbuilding that had a large case of old books; on top of it were piles of dust-covered tomes, which the servant nonchalantly threw down to the dealer. One, battered and held together with twine, looked particularly unpromising.

"That is no good," the servant sniffed. "Sir, it is only old poetry."

It was rather more than that.

"I unloosened the string," Railton writes, "opened the book, and saw at once what a treasure was found."

The world already had over a hundred known Folios; one more was a splendid find, but hardly earthshaking. What makes the Sibthorp Folio unique is a handwritten inscription across the top of the title page:

Ex dono Willi Jaggard Typographi. Ao 1623

It was, incredibly, a present from the Jaggards to one of their own authors—the first and only known presentation copy of a First Folio. The binding held together with twine was the original, and it revealed a stamped arms of Augustine Vincent, a heraldry author and staunch Jaggard friend and ally. Since William had died a couple of weeks before the book had even formally been declared published, this copy was, one expert declared, "beyond a doubt, one of the very first that came from the press"—a claim cemented when, upon measurement, it proved to be the largest uncut copy in the world, with a title-page portrait "in a condition of unexampled freshness." It had been crisply inked from what was then a brand-new plate.

Folger's agonies of desire upon hearing news of this discovery need hardly be imagined: here was a pristine Folio owned by a contemporary of Shakespeare's—owned by a friend of Jaggard's, no less. He *had* to have it. What, he inquired through a dealer, would be its price? OWNER REPLIES FIVE THOUSAND POUNDS, came back a terse cable, WHICH I TAKE TO BE PROHIBITIVE.

And that would have been prohibitive—a record amount—except that Folger very much wanted it. But he could not stand to be outmaneuvered.

Folger called the owner's bluff—how about £4,000?—whereupon Sibthorp called *his* bluff.

How about £5,000?

Folger accepted, then tried again to knock down the price at the last minute. *No sale,* Sibthorp replied—and back went the Folio into its case.

Back and forth the two went for the next four years. Folger might, quite reasonably, have believed that he was dealing with the sort of doddering old toff that, well, turns his library into a billiards room. What Folger did not know—in fact, what the Folger Library still does not know, *as I have found his copy and own it*—is that Sibthorp had acquired and read Sidney Lee's Folio census. Sibthorp knew he owned a truly extraordinary book. You will read Lee's census in vain to find any kind of signed copy, or a copy that is larger or better printed; indeed, you can read through much of it without even finding any original bindings. My copy of the census has Sibthorp's signature dashed onto the cover, and a note on page 16, where Lee notes, "The largest dimension of height assignable to any of the enumerated copies is 13½ in; the largest breadth is 8¾ in. Only one copy,—that belonging to Mr. Conigsby Sibthorp—exactly combines both superlative measurements." Sibthorp has underlined his own name and written at the bottom of the page, *Lincoln, found in granary.*

Sibthorp could wait—and wait, and wait—because he knew the offers would keep coming in higher and higher. The world wasn't printing any more original uncut Folios. For once, Folger was truly stumped: his new money couldn't just buy out old money. In fact, a mere £5,000 wouldn't do the trick anymore.

How about £6,000?

No, Sibthorp replied, because—do you know?—he rather liked the funny old book now and was inclined to keep it.

£8,000?

Sadly, no—and what was more, Sibthorp told the agent to stop sending offers, or, perhaps he could ask once a year—around the holidays, let's say. Finally, the old man relented a little. "I do not want to sell the book . . ." he wrote to the dealer. "[For] £10,000 I might be tempted to part with it."

Folger broke down and cabled his agent: BUY WITHOUT FAIL EVEN AT TEN THOUSAND CASH.

This time, Sibthorp said yes. It was just over a million in today's dollars, and by far the most that had ever been spent on a Folio.

Folger couldn't bring himself to trust anyone else with the volume; instead of having it shipped from England, he and his wife personally visited, and he carried it back to the United States in his briefcase. Upon their return, Folger was so brimming with pride over his purchase—which he promptly deemed Folio #1—that for once he actually ended his years of silence and wrote an article on it for *Outlook* magazine.

"We are carried at once back nearly three hundred years to the splendors and struggles of the reign of Elizabeth and James," the oilman wrote rapturously, "when poets sang a glorious note, full-throated, when felonies were punished by branding the hand that stole, and ears were shorn to discourage eavesdropping where royalty conferred."

He didn't get too carried away, mind you—he was still a businessman. Amid these reveries, he didn't dare reveal the astonishing price he'd paid for the book. In fact, you can read the article without the faintest hint that he *had* bought it, that it had ever been for sale, or indeed that it had even left England. But no matter: Folio #1's value to him was all too clear.

It was, Folger wrote, "the most precious book in the world."

And they still won't give it to me.

"Hmm," Betsy starts. "How long do you need to see it?"

"Not long," I promise.

Because I hear they burn real quick, she seems to be waiting for me to say. But I don't, and so after eyeing me carefully one more time, she nods.

"Instead of bringing it up to *you*, let's bring you to *it*."

"Okay." My eyes widen.

Let me explain.

The Folger Library has a bank vault. I say this because the first time I saw it, walking through the basement to talk with a staff member, I stopped in my tracks and stared dumbly at it. There it was: an enormously hinged metal door, at least seven feet high, probably weighing more than an SUV. It wasn't as if I'd never seen a giant Moser-locked bank-vault door before; it's just that I'd never seen one in a library.

Betsy leads me down a series of stairs, and to the door, and I avert my eyes as she disengages the lock and swings the massive thing open. She motions me inward wordlessly, then closes the door behind us. We are now locked in.

"That's quite a door," I marvel.

"It's for climate control," she says, before adding distantly, "and security."

Indeed. The Folger's collection is worth as much—probably more—than what most banks hold. Folio #1 is worth . . . what? Ten million? Twenty million? Eighty million? How much is the only presentation copy of the world's most treasured book worth? And that's not counting the seventy-eight other folios, nor the quarter million other old books as well. They need some guarding: when left to the vagaries of the outside world, Folios have had a habit of getting lost. Most of them have disappeared in the last four centuries, after all. Aside from getting sliced up by dealers, going down in ships, or getting incinerated in vast urban conflagrations, Folios also faced both neglect and theft.

There have always been a disconcerting number of Folios that nobody cared to keep track of until it was too late. I know from a single ticket stub in London's National Archives, for instance, that the recently bankrupted Liverpool auctioneer Joseph Crisp hit upon the profitable expedient in 1848 of raffling off a First Folio; but I do not know what happened next to that Folio. Then again, sometimes discovering their fate is even worse. One of the earliest alleged Folio purchases—by Spanish ambassador and theater aficionado Count Gondamar—was pursued without result for decades. But in 2000, Anthony West's inquiries turned up an extraordinary 1860 letter by historian Don Pascual Gayangos, informing a British Library staffer that he had visited the count's near-abandoned residence in the north of Spain in 1835 and found a garret with hundreds of books strewn across the floor. They bore the count's arms on their vellum covers and had been left exposed to the elements from open windows. Pausing to pick through the rubble, Gayangos wrote, "I recollect having picked up among others a fol. volume being Shakespeare's Comedies, Histories and Tragedies."

He was, he explained, too young to know its significance; when he returned years later to find the book, he discovered that garret of old books had been sold to local merchants as scrap paper. The Folio had been torn out page by page and handed out to the residents of Valladolid—wrapped with twine around parcels of fish and chunks of cheese.

These days, the problem is more often too *much* attention of the most unwanted variety. In the summer of 2008, an eccentric and little-known English dealer came to the Folger to have a First Folio appraised and was promptly accused of possessing one stolen in 1998 from the Durham University library in England. Nonsense, he claimed, *his* Folio was simply a lucky find in Cuba, where he had gone to woo a nightclub dancer—and, no, that is not the strange part of the story—and where this old book was given to him by, of all people, a former bodyguard to Fidel Castro. "I wouldn't have known the difference between a First Folio Shakespeare and a paper-back Jackie Collins," the suspect claimed. Perhaps, but it can't have helped his case that his home is only fifteen minutes from Durham University.

In fact, a Shakespeare First Folio is just about the lousiest loot in the world to steal. Folios are now the most minutely studied published works in history: thanks to Hinman we know their textual variants; and thanks to everyone from Dibdin to Anthony West we know their distinct bindings, the annotations in the endpapers, the tears in their pages, and their replaced leaves. A careful inventory of the Durham Folio's pages was performed in 1905, so a number of its identifying marks were well-known: there's a patched hole in the colophon, for instance; there's a broken clasp on the outside of the book; there's a specific annotation regarding *Troilus and Cressida*.

Because of obstacles like these, another theft of a First Folio—from the Williams College library in 1940—also ended disastrously. Four months after gaining entry with the forged papers of a ficti-tious "Professor Sinclair E. Gillingham" of Middlebury College, the thief turned himself in and fingered three conspirators. None of the four had ever graduated high school—and "Professor Gilling-ham" was, in fact, a shoe salesman. The reason for turning himself in? The Folio they'd stolen was hot enough to roast marshmallows over. Though this didn't exactly end their criminal careers, as Folio historian Harold Otness has noted: "The sentencing judge received a letter asking for leniency for the aircraft worker [of the gang] be-cause he was designing a special military plane."

Otness adds drily, "That letter was a forgery."

Betsy and I pass through a wood-paneled foyer that, I suspect, is any-thing but actual wood—perhaps a fireproof facsimile—then we turn into a room of spartan metal shelves. Of the three vault rooms, one is dedicated entirely to visual art; this book room, though, has row after row of very old books, most bearing the rich brown bindings of the sixteenth, seventeenth, and eighteenth centuries. Meters slowly mark away the temperature and the humidity, which the moisture of my breath is undoubtedly already disturbing. Keeping the environment around the books perfect has been one of the great challenges of the library; this whole floor, known as Level C, recently spent two years under reconstruction after puddles began forming on the floors; one Folger librarian later called the project "the nightmare of my career."

We walk to the back of the long room, and Betsy halts.

"Here," she points at the back wall. "These are the seventy-nine Folios."

I stand stock-still, amazed. I hadn't expected to see them all at once. They lie on their sides—not standing up, as I might have assumed—and are piled two and three high atop decidedly unglamorous off-white enameled metal shelving, the sort of thing you'd use in your garage. It takes up less space than you'd think. A hundred bucks at Target and you could probably shelve the entire world's supply of Folios.

Many of them are in rather similar red morocco bindings, but it's not Folger's.

"Oh, no," Betsy says, "none of those are rebound by us. The red bindings, that's just a very popular fashion from the nineteenth century."

I don't see the Vincent Folio; curious, I turn and look at the other books that surround us.

"This back here is all Shakespeare"—Betsy indicates a small section of the room—"but the rest of the shelves cover other eras and writers. It's only the Shakespeare that most people hear about."

"And Folio One?"

"Is here."

She indicates a table where the *first* First Folio has been laid out. It's dull brown, and it's huge—*huge*—the Motherfolio. At least, it's big if you're thinking in quarter inches. But the inscription inside this slab of leather and paper is actually quite small and neat. And it turns out, it's not the only writing. At some point a child penned in the letter *A* three times. There's something charming about "the most precious book in the world" being no match for some seven-year-old. In fact, we don't really know what happened to this book for most of its history; like most things, it was buffeted by the great constants of death and debt. We do know that after Vincent died, he left his books to a collector named Ralph Sheldon—and he, by one old account, took to "relieving several of his books that were pauned for ale."

God knows where it went from there.

These days, Folio #1 is closely watched; like the other Folger Folios, it has a file and a chart devoted to its every page; their layout bears a strange resemblance to a tournament chart, or an office football pool. There's now plenty of time to study each Folio, for the days of mad acquisition are long past. Folios generally follow new money, after all.

"So there's no modern-day Folgers snapping these up for the library, I guess?"

No, Betsy laughs, the obsessive modern collectors aren't over here.

"For that," she says, "you need to go to Japan."

ACT V

The Globe Theatre, Shin-Okubo, Shinjuku Ward

WHERE THE THEATER has stage darkness, life has darkness. To encounter true darkness in a theater is as unexpected as, say, an actual death onstage during a tragedy. The latter *can* happen, as in 1798 when actor John Palmer—some claimed—cried out his lines "Oh God! Oh God! There is another and a better world!"—and fell onto a Liverpool stage and off of our inferior planet. But darkness in a theater? That is rare.

Right now I cannot see a thing.

There are no lighted EXIT signs glowing in the darkness, no bulbs along the floor, no faint gels at the ready in the grid, nothing at all: there are, I am alarmed to realize, apparently no safety measures at all: just a faint polite murmur of a packed Tokyo house that cannot see the *Kabuku* programs in front of their faces. We have been plunged into darkness, and nobody knows quite what to expect.

What we do know is this: it is the opening run in this space of the Speedy Shocking Surprised Live theater company, the debut of a new play, the return to the stage of a pop idol, and quite possibly the strangest spectacle to ever play in a building bearing the name and design of the Globe.

It's not easy to find. First you have to set out from the Shin-Okubo station—green-striped trains blowing past in the night air, shimmery under the fluorescent station lights, the command of *Abunai desu kara, sawaranai de kudasai* floating behind you from PAs as you take the escalator down. The Tokyo Globe is up a long and drowsy street of vertical restaurant banners, patina-green hooded streetlamps, and ¥100 stores. It's not far from Kabukicho, the entertainment district that inspired the set design of *Blade Runner*. Yet this neighborhood is sleepier, with a respectable Koreatown of kimchi joints and K-pop shops hawking stickers and CDs and flickering electric light into the darkness.

The Globe is tucked among tower apartment blocks, like seemingly everything else here. It has no clear frontage, no marquee; you could walk right past without realizing, and in fact this is exactly what I do, wandering downstairs into a subterranean arcade signposted SHAKESPEARE ALLEY. The alley's primary tenant is a hair-and-nail salon that has been shuttered for the night. I clamber upstairs, going to the back of the theater by mistake. It takes a good many minutes of miming and broken English and Japanese, and a ticket seller's mysterious insistence that I am named Jason, before I finally wander in with my ¥6,800 ticket.

The Tokyo Globe bears its heritage lightly; just a few years before it opened in 1988, architect Arata Isozaki also created Studio 54's successor, the Palladium. The new Globe doesn't have mirror balls hanging from the ceiling, but it remains distinctly modern: the exterior is salmon-pink concrete, its circular shape achieved from a twenty-four-sided polygon, with a foundation built to isolate the building from the JR Yamanote rail line, whose trains rumble by scarcely fifty meters away. Inside, the walls are cornered into a decagon, with two balconies—a nice nod to the London original—and at its opening it even had a groundling area, a flat standing-room space below the stage for the cheap and rowdy multitude.

What those first crowds standing in the pit saw was an Ingmar Bergman stage production of *Hamlet*; the brooding mod protagonist used sunglasses to keep his eyes hidden from courtiers. Bergman? Why, yes—why not? The building and the production—the whole idea of building a Globe in Tokyo—all bubbled up in the speculative froth of Japan's 1980s economy. Van Goghs were bid up into the tens of millions, and golf club memberships were traded and listed in the papers like mutual funds, under the Nikkei Golf Club Membership Index. Even when the total market value of golf club memberships topped two hundred billion dollars, few saw an end coming. Follies were committed, and follies were built. A seventeenth-century Dutch village in Nagasaki! Greek temples on Shodoshima! A Spanish castle in Nagoya! Canadian World in Hokkaido! . . . *Canadian* World? . . .

No matter. So why not throw some millions into re-creating Shakespeare's theater in the middle of Tokyo? Why not bring your favorite Swedish movie director to produce your favorite Shake-speare play? Like Bergman, the building itself nods to the old the-atrical forms, but can't help trying to improve on the original: there's high-traffic carpeting, rounded and straight modern lines every-where, bright electronic track lights. Though it's perhaps not as much of a departure as the Globe replica that just opened this year in Sweden. That one was carved out of ice.

· · ·

Hai!

It begins: Kodo drumming behind a blue-lit scrim, dancing warriors sword-fighting with an ultra-amplified (((clang))) and (((whack))) worthy of *Batman*. The year is 1730: the shogunate is shaky, and a town is going awry. An aging courtesan in a splendiferous robe gets drunk on sake, cackling across the proscenium, while a bearded villain in old brown-plated armor uses a gramophone horn and tubing to wickedly control villagers with his martial voice. A Victorian dandy appears. An electric guitar is brandished as a weapon. So is a leaf-blower.

Kabuku is best described as a comedic-tragical-historical musical—which is to say, it is indescribable. The music cues veer wildly from cheesy *Doctor Who* synth flourishes to weepy piano ballads, to—unaccountably—a samurai break-dancing to C+C Music Factory. Then, just for the hell of it, they lurch into a parody of *Swan Lake*. These scenes are punctuated with thunderclaps of sound—a horse whinnying, say—that rattle your ribs loose. Then an explosion of flash pots sears your eyes out of their sockets.

"Izam!" Two girls hiss to each other from behind my seat. There is a whispered giggle. "*Izam!* Ho-ohhh!"

It's true: the pop idol Izam is the protagonist—such as there can be—in this impressively chaotic pile-up of a musical. He used to be Japan's answer to Boy George and emerged from several years of relative quiet to debut tonight as actor and composer for *Kabuku*. Izam still possesses just a hint of eyeliner and rouge about him; the crowd's women are delighted.

He won't be the first man in makeup to stride the boards here—not even the first pop star to—but Izam's show wasn't quite the original purpose behind the Tokyo Globe. After its opening in 1988, it hosted domestic companies performing Shakespeare plays in Japanese, and foreign touring companies like the RSC, often in straight-up Elizabethan English; audiences struggled gamely to follow, translated editions on their laps. From this came a flowering of Shakespeare productions: by 1990 seventeen different *Hamlet*s were playing across Tokyo alone. There was a *Broken Hamlet* of slackers in the sixth-century Asuka dynasty; a *Hamlet* built around a greengrocer's son; a Hong Kong underworld *Hamlet* shot through with references to the still-fresh massacre in Tiananmen Square; a *Heisei Rocky Hamlet* play-within-a-play of Japanese prisoners putting on a *Hamlet* production. You could, if you wished, have seen Laertes and Ophelia practicing tai chi onstage.

Hamlet and *King Lear* have long been close to the hearts of Japanese audiences—their agonized dilemmas of duty to the crown and of filial loyalty have a peculiarly strong resonance here—and Japan has a venerable tradition of staging Shakespeare, going back at least to an 1884 Bunraku puppet *Julius Caesar.* Before that, one must push back curtain after curtain of obscuring time: a Tokyo production *may* have derived from *Romeo and Juliet* in 1810, decades before Perry's "black ships" ended Japan's centuries of isolationism—and the Japanese *may* have procured this text in a Dutch translation from their sole trading partner, the Dutch East India Company, via the port of Nagasaki—and there *may* be faint echoes of *A Merchant of Venice* in a 1695 play by Chikamatsu, the "Japanese Shakespeare"—for there *may* have been a random quarto left by a ship called *The Globe* in 1613.

Well, the last is an absurd stretch of speculation—but a pleasing one.

And so the Tokyo Globe worked brilliantly; until it stopped working, at least. Hosting foreign companies in Tokyo doesn't come cheap; even full houses struggle under the expense. In 2002 this theater was sold to Johnny's Jimusho, a Tokyo outfit that managed *idoru* boy-band members. In a rather neat bit of jujitsu to the worst fears of old Globe fans, they staged a production of *Romeo and Juliet*—with a boy-band singer.

Izam's show lets out after two frenetic hours; emerging into the plazas and alleyways, the crowd mingles, chats, disperses into the streets of Shin-Okubo. I wander parallel to the train, following the tangles of power lines back to the station, pausing only to stop at the ranks of hot bottled tea and steel-canned coffee vending machines along the street corners. They're everywhere in Tokyo, wondrous things, their fronts flickering a mix of kanji and romaji characters out into the darkness, a constant interplay of English and Japanese: Pocari Sweat, Georgia Wild Drip, Fire Gold Rush, Boss Midnight Blend—the latter seemingly bearing the visage of Ernest Hemingway smoking a pipe. I down a Royal Milk Tea, lean against a traffic barrier, and flip open my cell phone to its electric-blue light. I kept it off for the entire *Kabuku* performance, and now a message awaits me: in the morning I will meet the world's greatest living dealer in Shakespeare First Folios.

SCENE ii.

Shinjuku Ward, Tokyo

JUST PAST EIGHT A.M., the crosswalks outside Shinjuku station are slick with rain and in full commuter roar: the painted lines are the size of a football field, with thousands pouring across every minute. Everyone's charging ahead purposefully; up above them, towering steel monoliths prop up billboards broadcasting Canon and Suntory into the rain. But everyone's looking down and ahead into Shinjuku. The labyrinthine structure has over two hundred entrances—all of them, it seems, leading into the same subway car. When you see pictures of salarymen being pushed by conductors into packed subway cars—that's Shinjuku. It's the busiest railway station in the world, with 3.6 million riders daily.

I keep checking my watch—I don't want to be late for the dealer, but I've made it to the station too early to want to deal with rush hour—and so I'm drawn down the street. I swim upstream against a sea of umbrellas, past shoals of vending machines, and across the booming Manboo manga cafés. A crowd is forming a couple blocks down, and this one isn't for the next Keio express. They're gathered by a towering green storefront labeled GREEN PEAS. Or, rather:

Green Peas WORLD.
COLLEGE • MUSEUM
10 YEN SLOTS • SLO-YOKO

This not entirely edifying sign is flanked on both sides, appropriately, by giant green fiberglass peapods.

"What *is* this?" I ask an old man smoking nervously at the edge
of the sidewalk. A Mazda just misses his foot.

"The game." He mimes turning the pinball handles. "Pachinko."

It's a pachinko parlor. Technically illegal, yet practically every-
where: people are already lining up for parlors that won't open until
ten. The best seats are supposed to be by the front window, so they're
now all engaged in a variant of the ancient and honorable game of
Greater Fool: who is the greater fool, the man who shows up late
and misses the best machines, or the one who got out of a warm
bed early to play pachinko?

I wander on, gathering names of stores. It is impossible for an English speaker not to delight in a country where the same block contains both Freshness Burger and the Chin Goo restaurant. Store My
Ducks. Junk Jewel! Love Hippy. Ciao Panic! Stores crazily blossom
signage up and down, diagonal and spiraling and flashing; shops are
largely above or below streets, intensely vertical, so that the ground is
purely kinetic—for moving from one skyward or subterranean nest
to another—with all the life and contemplation of the city occurring
either over your head or under your feet.

It is almost a relief to enter the thousand-foot rapids of Shinjuku
station. I am sluiced down concourses, flooded through gates, poured
into a train to Akebono-Bashi, and minutes later washed up on

Sanei-cho, on the steps leading up to the second-floor entrance to the Yushodo Company Ltd.

It's fitting that the first thing an antiquarian shop should confront you with, right in its vestibule, are books. Just inside Yushodo's there's an open case of old, worn-out *Punch* volumes from the 1840s, filled with fanciful sketches and mock ads: "TO BE PARTED WITH, for the veriest trifle, a LONG ESTABLISHED COLD, of a sonorous, deep-toned quality." It's an unimaginable distance for London humor magazines—so of their time and place, some winter's day in Fleet Street—to find them on a quiet Tokyo avenue nearly two centuries later. They're something that you might not notice upon entering the shop, but *Punch* has a curious role in Japanese literature. *Punch* inspired *Japan Punch*, the country's first magazine, launched in Yokohama in 1862. The inimitable cartoon work of *Punch* helped mold a generation of Japanese cartoonists, the ancestors of today's manga artists. Digging out these random old magazines, foxing themselves in the vestibule window, is like holding up a fossil from a branch of modern Japan's literary evolution. A Triassic fern, perhaps.

Shakespeare, too, underwent a wondrous change upon these shores. His first rendering in Japanese was, fittingly, in an 1871 cartoon in *Japan Punch*: it shows a sword-wielding samurai deep in contemplation, musing, *Arimas, arimasen, are wa nan deska*—a ludicrously rough translation of "To be or not to be, that is the question." From that first frame of his existence here as a samurai Hamlet, Shakespeare's been peculiarly Japanese. Long before Western directors were outdoing each other to transmute Shakespeare's times and settings, the Japanese adapted him so fearlessly that their productions were entirely new creations of art.

It couldn't have been an easy task. Japanese theater did not draw upon Western notions of realism, veering instead between exaggeration in drama and infinite reserve in tender emotions; the playwright Kinoshita Junji once mocked the latter with this wordless set of stage directions:

> MAN. *(Looks longingly at the woman.)*
> WOMAN. *(Looks longingly at the man.)*
> MAN. *(Tries to say something.)*
> WOMAN. *(Tries to say something.)*
> MAN. *(Is choked with emotion.)*
> WOMAN. *(Is choked with emotion.)*
> MAN. *(Tries to move his lips.)*
> WOMAN. *(Tries to move—)*

To build a production around an alien acting style that few Japanese had ever seen would have been nearly impossible; instead, Shakespeare had to be made Japanese. That's why Japan's first stage production of Shakespeare in 1885 was not actually a Shakespearean play called a *Merchant of Venice*—because, to begin with, it was now a kabuki, and no longer set in Venice. *Merchant* became *Life Is as Fragile as Cherry Blossoms in a World of Money*—Venice became Osaka—Shylock became Stubborn Tightfist—and 1598 became 1854, with the markets of Japan being thrown open by the American black ships.

Everything is changed; yet it is somehow the same.

A World of Money begins, incredibly, with Japanese college students arguing whether the production they are about to see will civilize them into Western life. *A World of Money* came out when westernization was powerfully confronting Japan, alongside a popu-

lar tract titled *Datsu-a ron*—"Japan Must Transcend Asianness."
The significance of art and of nationalism does not just lurk in the
background of this play. It literally steps in front of it and addresses
the audience, in the persons of the arguing students:

> NAKAMURA: Western novels are surely superior to Chi-
> nese or Japanese novels in their high spiritual and
> moral standards. Yet, it seems to me, Chinese and
> Japanese novels are better in that they are more
> entertaining than Western ones.
>
> WADA: I disagree. Western novels might seem less enter-
> taining, but it is because our taste is not totally civi-
> lized. In the West, because people's minds are
> civilized, they do not want savage, superstitious,
> and barbaric entertainments from their novels. On
> the other hand, Asians only seek savage and supersti-
> tious entertainment from their novels. So for us
> Japanese, who are *han-kai* [half-civilized], Western
> novels seem to be less entertaining.

The recognition that Shakespeare was a byword for prestigious
Western art meant that putting on any of his plays was also considered a mark of cultural progress. And *A World of Money* was popular: at least twelve different productions were staged in Japan in the
late 1800s, to be followed by kabuki versions of *King Lear*, *Othello*,
Timon of Athens, and *The Taming of the Shrew*.

Perhaps even more people saw the serializations of Shakespeare
that ran in newspapers; the *Hamlet* adaptation *Hamuretto Yamato
Nishiki-e* that appeared in *Tokyo Eiri Shimbun* in 1886 trades Denmark for Japan, has Laertes commit suicide, and features stunningly

beautiful woodblock illustrations. To look at this *Hamuretto*—Claudius a fierce kabuki warrior, Polonius white-haired and cross-eyed, and a beseeching Ophelia in the frozen *mei* pose—you would swear that you were reading a classic Japanese text. Which, in fact, you are.

The bard was born in Stratford—and he was reborn here.

Mitsuo Nitta may be the world's foremost First Folio dealer, but he is also a publisher; a maker, you might say, of antiquarian books of the future. The interior of his Yushodo Company Ltd. is alive with old books, but Nitta—a graying, dignified man, clearly proud of his great collection—above all wants to show me a new book.

"This is a collection of *washi*." He passes me a heavy, smooth folding *chitsu* box containing three volumes bound in *waso* fabric and secured with clasps crafted of green ribbon and little wooden dowels that fit into two loops. The *washi* inside are beautiful hand-made Japanese papers, tactile sheets of inset flowers and ferns—and this is a directory of makers, with their contact information printed on a page of their own paper.

"Very special paper," he says. "Four hundred years pass, nothing changes. Paper stays the same."

I leaf past pages of delicate tissue and marvel at a sheet of twin-woven paper.

"It seems easier to find well-preserved books from four hundred years ago than a hundred years ago. It's not just our modern paper, it's the bindings, too. Modern glue bindings won't hold up like this *waso* will."

Nitta nods. He has also published in white vellum bindings, which are nearly unheard of in our era. It's a premodern technique using untanned hides, but one that creates astonishingly strong bindings that can last for millennia.

"Very expensive." He smiles at the memory of it. "It is hard to find binders who will do it."

"I've noticed," I venture, "that old Japanese books tend to survive the centuries better than old English ones."

"You have been looking at many Folios in your search?"

"Yes—they're not always as handsome as these books."

"They have their beauty. But it is a difficult time to sell Shakespeare. The trade, it is driven by individuals. A Gates or a Getty— when they are buying, prices go up. But right now . . ." Nitta shrugs. "A good time to buy. Not much competition. If you want a Folio now, you can probably ask twenty-five, thirty percent off from a dealer."

"But it didn't used to be like that."

"Oh, no! It was very different twenty years ago."

"How did the buying begin in Japan?"

"Well . . ." he settles back in his chair, adjusts his steel spectacles, and gazes into the past. "You know of Mitsuo Kodama?"

Indeed I do—or I know of the name, at least—the late president of Meisei, a large university outside Tokyo that few Westerners had heard of—and I've heard whispers of his intermediaries quietly manning book auctions in his name. Beyond that, little seems to be known of Kodama, save his mysterious connection to many, many Folios.

"Kodama visits the UK, hmm, forty years ago," Nitta leans forward. "And he meets rare-book specialists at the British Library. He wants to collect, but what? And one of the specialists suggests to him, 'You should collect Shakespeare.'" Nitta is warming to his subject. "And . . . that's it! This is what gives him the idea. First he buys a

Second Folio. He also becomes friends with a professor of medieval and Renaissance studies in Maryland. This professor agrees to give Kodama his Second, Third, and Fourth Folios when he dies."

By "give," I think he really means *give*—and not sell. And by "die," I think he means—well, *die*. At some point, every book collector becomes keenly aware of their own mortality, as they are the recipients of books that have passed through collection after collection, long literary lines of succession. Collectors simply curate their books for a next generation to acquire, and to then pass on as well.

"So Kodama is waiting, waiting—ten years he waits. But then Kodama acquires some money from some land he owns. Land prices are going up then, in the early 1970s."

"The real estate bubble?"

"Yes. And now he has—in today's currency—about three million dollars."

Nitta's fingers spread to indicate the collection, the hundreds of millions of yen, the glorious expanding metropolis before us.

"Kodama decides," he adds, "to start buying Folios and quartos."

Even before Kodama's fateful advice from the British Library, Japan had spent the twentieth century priming itself for something like this to happen. After the early efforts at Shakespeare in woodblocks and kabuki, by the turn of the twentieth century visiting Japanese actors were beginning to actually see traditional productions in Europe, and they returned home with newfangled notions of realism. Thanks in part to Otojiro Kawakami—songwriter, actor, occasional umbrella salesman, and all-around barnstorming reformer and artist—*Hamlet* in particular proliferated across Japan. It could take new titles like *The Maple Leaf Palace*, using a traditional *onnagata* female impersonator for Gertrude, and even jettisoning soliloquies—which at first struck Japanese playwrights as downright peculiar—but the productions filling Tokyo in the first decade of the 1900s were getting recognizably closer to Western realism. Such was the zeal of these *shimpa* (new school) players to re-create the West that, incredibly, they'd perform Shakespeare in what can only be called whiteface—by sporting blue eye shadow and flared prosthetic noses. For the next fifty years kabuki Shakespeare essentially ceased, and *Hamlet* and other plays began appearing as full-text renditions: productions that Shakespeare himself would have recognized, even without understanding a word of them.

And so the cult grew: a Shakespeare Association of Japan formed in 1929, and the bard was regarded with enough fondness that, even with the Sino-Japanese Wars in the 1930s pouring nationalist fervor into Japan's ears like a vial of poison, Shakespeare long escaped the censure upon foreign art. One of the very last Shakespeare productions before World War II was a comedy—*Twelfth Night*—staged in March 1938 by an all-female cast in, of all places, the Military Club of Tokyo. If officers saw anything remiss in watching a comedy—or an English play—they did not say so.

Even when Shakespeare ceased altogether during the war, hints of a quiet scholarly love for the plays still occasionally peeped out. Writing heavily of impending war in his 1940 book *Shakespeare in Japan*, the scholar Toyoda Minoru pleaded with readers to remember their common humanity. "During the last Great War," he recalled, "the annual reports of the Shakespeare society in Germany were not discontinued . . . Is it not in mutual understanding and spiritual brotherhood that the final hope of humanity reposes?"

The following year the Shakespeare Association was dissolved, and Tokyo's leading actor of Hamlet thrown in jail. But if the government was hoping to weed out foreign influences, it was decades too late. The seed was already planted for Kodama's generation.

"Here is a catalog we published in 1980," Nitta tells me, showing me a volume of Meisei's holdings. "Remember that Kodama begins collecting in 1975. By 1980 they already have four First Folios."

With the presidency of Meisei University—and control of its library's acquisitions—Kodama's reach became almost supernatural. In the 1970s and 1980s Folios suddenly disappeared from the auction houses of America and Europe, and nobody knew where they were going. Who on earth was buying all the world's Folios?

"There are more Meisei volumes," Nitta adds, "another in 1986, and again in 1993. To account for the growth of the collection."

By the time Kodama died, one room in suburban Tokyo held twelve First Folios—more than the British Library and the New York Public Library *combined*. Meisei is now second only to the mighty Folger Library in the world's holdings of First Folios.

"How involved were you in all this?"

"Kodama buys . . . ah . . . about fifty-seven various Folios and quartos," Nitta tallies. "I am involved in about ninety percent of these purchases."

"That's extraordinary."

"Come"—he smiles—"I will show you more."

Nitta and I stroll through his six-story premises—at seventy-six years old, it's one of the city's older antiquarian shops—and the care with which the place has been laid out is only slowly unfolding to me. On the top floor he shows me a reference library of books on books, perfectly selected—"Duyckinck!" I almost shout, and lift up a weighty volume with glee, so far from its antebellum origins in

Manhattan. Nitta consults all these in his dealings, and scholars also come by to use them. Some of his treasures, though, are kept away from prying eyes. In the Rare Book Room off his lobby, he opens a box filled with old documents and passes me a typescript marked up with comments.

"Have a look at this," he smiles.

I stare blankly; it takes a moment to sink in.

"This is a Henry Miller manuscript."

"Yes."

"Where on earth do you find something like this?"

"Oh, I buy them from Henry Miller's wife."

"She's . . . still around?"

"Oh, yes! She is Japanese, did you know? When he was seventy, he married her, and she was forty-eight years younger." He relates this last fact with a hint of wonderment, even admiration.

The soul of his business still comes from these kinds of personal contacts—although the books themselves go to the highest bidder at auction, before and afterward it is all a matter of cultivating relationships. Yet that part of the business may also be slipping into the past. His company has been expanding, but the specter of the obsolescence of the antiquarian trade looms. Internet price comparisons have hurt the trade.

"And then there's Stanford, Columbia," he says. "They are putting their rare books online, digitizing them in the next decade with Google. Fewer people will need originals in the future."

Antiquarian dealing, if not a dying trade, may at least be a contracting one.

"I have a meeting with Amazon today," he eases the Miller typescript back into its case. "We try to work with the future."

"And this business in the future"—I motion to furnishings all around us—"is this a family concern? Will another Nitta be in charge?"

No, he shakes his head.

"I have no successor yet," he says.

I pause a moment, look back at the *washi* volumes, then at Nitta.

"Now that Kodama is no longer—no longer among us—what do you think will happen to the Folios?"

"Yes," he muses. "A good question. There is much conflict at Mei-sei, by librarians. They think too much money was spent buying First Folios." He has contacted them asking them if they want to sell the Folios—and they do want to, by his account. "I even had a collector offering one million dollars for a Folio. And they might like to sell. But they cannot sell."

"Why not?"

"They are twenty percent funded by the government. So it is in part the government's."

He leans back a little and smiles. This is not the real problem, he says.

"So what's really stopping them?"

"The problem is . . . ah. If a university sells a book, it *makes a rumor*—that they need money, are out of money. And so they will not sell."

"Even if they don't want the book anymore?"

"No," he shakes his head. "To do so would be seen as a sign of weakness."

It is a stunning admission, and yet it makes a curious kind of sense. As with so much here, there is a paramount concern with politely saving face. If there were a way to sell a First Folio without anyone

noticing, maybe they would—but when you own one of the most famous books in the world, someone *will* notice—and so they cannot.
Meisei owns twelve extraordinarily rare books that they are not entirely sure they want, but that they're quite sure they can't be seen
to *not* want.

Nitta, a book lover at heart, sees the humor in the situation.

"The Meisei librarians don't want to talk about having the First
Folios. They feel conflicted about them." He smiles. "But their scholars are *delighted*."

Meisei University, Hino, Tokyo

MEISEI UNIVERSITY LOOKS out commandingly over the suburb of Hino, like a hilltop fortress. Ascending the long and winding covered walkway feels curiously lonely at this time of day. Everything about Meisei bespeaks a population of thousands, and yet it's just me and Professor Michiro Yabuki walking up the hillside, and the hum of the Tama local train sliding away behind us. With the dying off of the train's roar, I hear the sound of construction and see showers of sparks up ahead; two new buildings are going up at Meisei's campus; one will rise fourteen stories over the surrounding landscape.

Yabuki, an affable, middle-aged computer-science professor at Meisei, folds his trench coat over his arm, runs a hand through his Einsteinian shock of graying hair, and smiles as he regards the bristling steel hulk.

"My new departmental office will be in there," he says.

Meisei is growing—and fast.

An imposing series of concrete and steel and glass honeycombed buildings, only given away by the word MEISEI written in flowerbeds across the hillside, there is nothing in the appearance of this campus that would lead you to expect a Folio—not even one, let alone twelve.

But of that dozen, there is a specific copy—the Meisei Folio—that I have truly come to see.

"So"—I gesture toward the cranes and hard hats—"this will be the building that will broadcast the Meisei Folio to the world."

"Yes," he laughs. "You could say."

It's not the first time Yabuki has worked closely with books. Back in the 1990s, he translated computer books into Japanese—including, I'm delighted to learn, one titled *Programming with Curses*. Alas, Curses turns out to simply be a UNIX function.

"Did you ever think you'd be working on a project like this one?"

Yabuki considers this a moment, and we stroll uphill toward the Shakespeare Hall theater and the Kodama Memorial Library. He always had an eye on Western art, he says, even when growing up.

"I own two Gibson guitars. I grew up in the Beatles generation, with the West Coast sound. Janis Joplin! And I like Oscar Wilde." For a moment, they both sound like headliners at the Fillmore.

"But," he adds, "I would not have guessed Shakespeare."

Shakespeare has always been close to the heart of modern Japanese universities. While *The Merchant of Venice* may have been the first play to appear onstage in Japan, it wasn't the first to get translated; that honor went to *Julius Caesar* in 1884, when it was translated into *The Strange Story of Caesar: The Renowned Sharpness of the Blade of Liberty*. The translator was an amazing polymath known universally as Shoyo—his birth name was Tsubouchi Yuzo, but much as urbane European authors during the Enlightenment liked to adopt Latin pseudonyms, modern Japanese reformers and sophisticates liked to take Chinese names. And so it was Shoyo who, wandering the University of Tokyo library, happened to pick up a complete English edition of Shakespeare. The first play he opened it to was

Julius Caesar, and it read uncannily to him, for just a month earlier the political boss Hoshi Tōru had been assassinated in Tokyo City Hall. It was, perhaps, a sign. Shoyo went to work.

Over the next fifty years Shoyo would eventually translate all of Shakespeare's works, but in that first play he found himself facing some unique challenges. Along with such alien notions as soliloquies, the poetry, the English system of meter and accent, didn't make much sense in Japanese. Their poetry relied on syllable count and changes in pitch and used five- and seven-syllable lines—not an easy task when, say, a character like Malvolio hogs up four syllables every time his name is uttered. Japanese pronunciation also kept character names from tripping off the tongue; as Japanese words are consonant-vowel, and because of the confoundment of *R* and *L*, Hamlet became *Hamuretto*, and Shakespeare himself turned into *Sheikusupia*.

Shoyo's solution to all this? Puppets.

Or rather, Bunraku, an ancient Japanese dramatic form acted out with wooden puppets. The lyrical conventions of Bunraku suited themselves handily to Shakespeare—and so *Julius Caesar* became a Bunraku-style written work. To Shoyo, this made perfect sense: as one scholar has noted, we know more about fourteenth-century Bunraku than we do about how Richard Burbage acted out *Caesar* three hundred years later. Japanese theater provides directors with a more stable theatrical tradition to build upon than English theater ever did.

Led by a generation of University of Tokyo students trained by resident Western professors like Lafcadio Hearn, Japanese scholars rather came to regard Shakespeare as their own—one early student even quoted *Hamlet* in his suicide note, before a fatal plunge into a waterfall—and the logical extreme finally came in 1915 when the scholar Takataro Kimura called the man an invention of Japan itself.

Kimura's pamphlet *Shakespeare's Hamlet and Its Oriental Materials* declared, "*Hamlet* from top to toe is composed of Oriental, or exclusively Japanese, materials . . . [It is] nothing but a medley and patching of Oriental materials, and therefore we need not acknowledge the genius of Shakespeare." His theory didn't find many takers—the idea of a plagiaristic journey of *Hamlet* from Edo-era Japan to Renaissance England is charmingly fanciful—but Kimura's eccentric notions were a sign of just how deeply tied Shakespeare's work was becoming to Japanese tradition.

More respectable efforts at Shakespeare biography and criticism would follow, but the epitome of Japanese scholarship remains one of its earliest works: Kochi Doi's 1929 essay *Sheikusupia to Hana* (Shakespeare and the Flowers). Doi brought a Japanese eye to Shakespeare's works, and what he noticed were . . . flowers. The highly stylized and deliberative philosophy of flower arranging known as *ikebana* is an art form in Japan. Only a Japanese scholar would have bothered to look for significance in the flowers of Shakespeare, yet significance is what he found. While skeptical Western scholars busied themselves with buried cryptograms and arcane references to the playwright in public records, Doi simply pointed out what was hidden in plain sight.

The flowers in Shakespeare's plays, he noted, were the ones that grew around Stratford-upon-Avon.

Yabuki and I have been joined by his young English-department colleague Professor Noriko Sumimoto—"I must show you our Shakespeare Hall!" she tells me, so we wander through a three-hundred-seat, modern theater built again around the Globe's model, our steps echoing off the stage into the darkness—and as we make our way around the campus English offices and to library officials, tea is offered at every stop. Despite my having already slugged down too many Kilimanjaro 100s from canned-coffee machines, it seems impolite not to drink the proffered cups—particularly because it feels important to do so. I do not actually know yet whether I'll be seeing a Folio; drinking tea over a polite conversation is the Japanese equivalent of an application process.

By the time I reach Kodama Memorial Library to meet the rare-books curator, I'm wired liked an electrical substation.

"*Ohayo gozaimasu,*" he says, and bows.

"HELLO!" I jangle his hand up and down.

Despite this, the assembled officials decide to lead me to their book vault.

Most of the library is a regular hangout for working students, and the first table I pass has a *Rolling Stone* back issue at the ready among a pile of sober textbooks; the cover announces "The Passion of Kanye West." But deep inside Kodama Memorial, things look a little different; a spookily half-lit section of metal shelving is filled with Shakespeare crit, and just beyond that lies an unobtrusive side door. And it will not open if you tug on it.

After some slightly guarded ministrations and supplications to the security system, the curator ushers us in, and the fluorescent lights flicker on. Like the Folger Library, the Kodama library maintains a windowless and fireproof book vault, where its most precious books reside in cryptlike cool and dry air, perpetually monitored for temperature and humidity. But unlike the Folger—which really does look like a storage vault—Kodama built his vault as a pleasant reading room with a long wooden conference table, oak shelving, and the books arranged with the idiosyncratic feel of a professor's house. The Folger has the vault of a cultural institution; the Kodama has the vault of a cultured man.

As soon as I walk in, a book on a shelf of small pocket editions from the eighteenth and nineteenth centuries catches my eye: *Robt E Lee's Shakespeare. London, 1832.*

"Is that," I ask, a little stupidly, because I cannot conceive of its referring to anyone else, "*General* Robert E. Lee?"

They are not sure.

It is drawn down from the shelf; I open it up, and sure enough, there's the general's own signature on the title page. It is his copy of *Julius Caesar.* Kodama was a wide-ranging collector, and the room is filled with such riches: signed editions of Twain, an 1817 first edition of Keats, first editions of Dickens—and *barely anyone knows this place exists.*

Naturally, there is every edition of Shakespeare imaginable. The first complete edition to supersede the Folios is here, of course, and Sumimoto hands me the 1709 edition by Nicholas Rowe and published by Jacob Tonson. Their opening illustration for *The Tempest* is still as sharp and clear as the day it was published, with lightning zigzagging across the ship masts. Modern photography means that today artists draw lightning as branching, organic; but in Rowe it's still at wicked, demonic angles, all shattered pitchforks and flying razors.

"Have a look at this one." Professor Sumimoto draws down a stout volume and hands it to me gingerly. It's a folio, in an original binding, and includes a dedication by Henry Holland, a preface by Ben Jonson, and—the binding looks like a First Folio—it clearly *is* a first folio. But there's a difference:

The Workes of Benjamin Jonson

London,

Printed by WILLIAM STANSBY

M. DC. XVI.

It's the very model for Shakespeare's own folio, printed the year William passed away. Leafing through preliminary pages, I am arrested by a single annotation.

"This one is *signed* by Jonson."

But they've already moved on to the next treasure and are beaming over it. As I have been reading, Yabuki and Sumimoto have been bustling about with quiet enthusiasm, taking one volume after another off the shelves. When I look back up, I find they have opened First, Second, Third, and Fourth Folios, laying them out along the long conference table, along with a 1532 Chaucer, and a gap for the Ben Jonson. I open the Jonson to its title page and set it down into the gap. I now have before my eyes something I have never seen before, and will likely never see again: a complete lineage of the First Folio, of its direct ancestors and immediate descendants.

I start at the far end, with Chaucer. Surprisingly, it wasn't until 1532 that William Thynne assembled a truly recognizable edition of Chaucer's works—the very first first folio—creating a precedent for the collections of Jonson and Shakespeare to follow nearly a century later. I turn the large pages in my hands, marveling at the thick and fussy black-letter typeface: it's striking to look at because you can see that they were still trying to use printing to mimic manuscript writing. Fonts had not become their own technology; they were still conceived of in the clumsy terms of a previous generation. We're not so different in our own century: our descendants might find it quaint that for a few generations we stubbornly clung to the notion of computers using pages and scrolls.

The Second, Third, and Fourth Folios all retained the heft of the First, though over the decades the title-page portrait became imperceptibly crisper in its lines, as each new generation performed a bit of cosmetic surgery on their bard. But the First Folio is not only unimproved, it is also unadorned. This is an almost blindingly rare sight: it is not just in a seventeenth-century binding, but its original 1623 binding. It is entirely unornamented in the way that only originals are, a manner that no later binder dares assay the modesty of; we hold Shakespeare in too high a regard to give him his original binding back, to see him as his compatriots did. Today, and for the past three hundred years, a First Folio has demanded red morocco and gold lettering on the spine, and tooled designs across the front. When you come across a folio that looks brown and scarred like a hard-used piece of wood—that's an original. The understatedness is their charm. This, relying solely on the words inside, is how they came into the world, without any gold leaf or luxury to herald them. In the beginning, there were only the words.

And the words are pretty damn odd.

One by one, more First Folios come out, covering the table. In front of me is the greatest collection of Folios within seven thousand miles—perhaps $50 million worth of Folios, and together they'd stack no higher than a first-grader. You could fit them—*not that you would*—into a single duffel bag. But one particular copy in its original binding—known as the Meisei Folio—is among the most prized of all Folios, and not just for its original binding, or because its owner, apparently a nephew of Ben Jonson's, wrote this in the outer margin of Ben's commendatory verse:

To the Memory of
My Uncel ye
author

No, it's what's written on the other pages—on all the other pages. The Meisei Folio is absolutely *crawling* with annotations: annotations up

the margins, annotations down the center gutter, annotations between the lines, annotations arching over the titles at the tops of
the pages and stuffed into the interstices between every bit of type
and leading. It's the only existing Folio that was heavily annotated
by its original owner.

I turn to act 3, scene 4 in *King John*:

> *extreame grief and shame for losse in warre*
> *desperat and vehement desire of death as the onely*
> *remeed of endlesse miseries of a passionat woman*
>
> *armado defeat and scattered*
> *victorie at full*
>
> *If men see and know their friends in heauen*
> *way giuen to grief in extreame miserie*
> *deceits of fortune*
>
> *loue in miserie and to*
> *the miserable*
>
> *lust reproaches and threats against an Impious*
> *sowlelesse cardinall legat*
>
> *loue of parents to oppressed children*
>
> *Tedeous life in miserie*
> *false shewes of deceiuable fortune*
> *Losse in shamefull Winning*

All this is within the margins of a single page; the reader's notes are
jammed line by line into margins, though read all together at once
they make their own strange poetry. And what's more, the reader was

also underlining the text—constantly, almost comically—so much that on this page of *King John* almost every single line has been completely underscored. At first glance, the Meisei Folio looks like the worst used textbook in a college bookstore, the one that some dope highlighted and underlined every page of. But it is proof of something much more: that in those early years after the Folio was published, when Shakespeare was just another pretty playwright, *somebody* out there was obsessive enough about his work to read every single line in nine hundred folio pages.

The Meisei Folio is unique in not only having a comprehensive annotator, but in also having a comprehensive *annotator of the annotator*. After this Folio's purchase in August 1980, Professor Akihiro Yamada went to view his university's new find.

"My first look . . . struck me with awe," he later recalled. "Because nearly every page of it, from cover to cover, was full of marginal notes in an extremely neat secretary hand of the seventeenth century. I had never come across such a book, small or large, blessed by such a diligent and devoted reader. Certainly the author of these annotations was, in the true sense of the word, one of the greatest lovers of Shakespeare."

Professor Yamada's transcription of these annotations was published in a 1998 volume, and the book bespeaks a monklike devotion to its subject. Along with transcribing every comment and mapping them to each page—he divides each leaf into six numbered sectors—he also created a concordance for the comments, tallied them in each play, *and* developed a spreadsheet of calculations to compare Shakespeare's word count to the annotator's. *King John* weighs in with 1,324 annotator's words to the bard's 17,748—a percentage, Yamada is careful to inform us, of 7.459. Our annotator greatly favored histories and tragedies, with a comedy like *The Merry Wives of Windsor* warranting just 201 annotations to Shakespeare's 21,119 words —or, I should say, 0.951 percent. The last time I saw such Shakespearean number-crunching was also in Japan—in the paper "The Time Allowed for Exits in Shakespeare's Plays," which applied a stopwatch and a calculator to *Hamlet* to fathom via pages of statistics exactly how Shakespeare managed his actors onstage.

Naturally, Yamada himself was modest about his work. "Shamefully," he wrote, "I confess that I have not read Shakespeare with as much care and industry as this seventeenth-century reader."

In fact, Yamada discovered a great many clues. First, while the Meisei Folio bears the bookplates of various nobles and well-heeled bibliophiles—twentieth-century übercollectors A. S. Rosenbach and Arthur Houghton both possessed it, and before them the tome passed through the hands of a Chicago millionaire and Scottish country squires—after the title page there is a more subtle inscription, in fading brown ink along the top:

William Johnstoune • • his Booke

Johnstoune and Jonson, thanks to the fluid nature of the spelling of last names, were part of the same extended family in the Dumfriesshire area of Scotland. Yamada also noticed that the owner's word choices—*agains* for "against," *nor* for "than," *propone* for "propose"—were distinct to Scotland during this time. Yet he didn't use possessive apostrophes or Italianate pen flourishes, both of which came into wider use by midcentury. Given the 1623 publication date, that meant these annotations likely date to the 1620s and 1630s. So by dint of careful observations, Yamada deduced that the likely first owner in the 1620s and 1630s was a Scotsman named

William Johnstoune, who was perhaps related to Ben Jonson. Beyond that, no scholar has been able to go any further.

But I have a guess.

There *is* a man, lost to obscurity for centuries, who fits Yamada's description: William Johnstone, professor of mathematics at the University of Aberdeen from 1626 to his death in 1640. Not only is he in the right region at the right time—and within the usual variability in surname spellings—he also came from a more literary background than the title "mathematics" might imply. The brother of poet and Psalms translator Arthur Johnstone, William was highly esteemed as a poet in his own right—"his skill in Latine was treuly Ciceronian," one chronicler recalled, and the great polymath Sir Thomas Urquhart praised him as "a good poet in Latine, and a good mathematician." Prior to his job in Aberdeen, Johnstone lived in Spain and taught philosophy in Germany; surviving student notes of his lectures at the University of Aberdeen show an impressively worldly range of knowledge, with one class entailing everything from arithmetic and Euclid to ecclesiastical math—the dating of Creation, for instance—as well as cosmology, geography, hydrography, surveying, and astronomy. His death in 1640 was much mourned, though perhaps not unexpected—he was, a colleague recalled, "a corpulent man, and a sanguinean; he was tackne awaye to the greate greefe of his freends and acquiantance." His personal library was impressive enough that many of his books were bequeathed to bulk up the University of Aberdeen's own holdings.

The markings and sheer use of the Meisei Folio are typical of a working scholar, for whom a new book is not an object to be dusted and displayed, but rather a crate of ideas to be pried open with the point of a pen; it is the book of a man with piles of volumes on his desk and marginal notes and queries on every page to himself, to the author, and to no one in particular. Given the sheer volume and doggedness of his writing, we now may be able to bestow upon Professor Johnstone a signal honor: he is the world's first scholarly reader of Shakespeare. The three of us in this vault are merely continuing what Johnstone began four centuries ago.

"Here is the secret website," Professor Yabuki jokes as we enter his office. Amid the whirr of multiple PCs and yet more tea—my cup is chattering against my saucer—Professor Sumimoto and I watch as Yabuki fires up his computer. "When the program to digitize the Folios was launched in 2001, at first we believed the programming would be contracted out," Yabuki continues. "But we found that this would be very expensive. So I began to program the website software myself."

"You coded a custom Folio-reading program?"

"Yes," he smiles. "It is a handmade website. But it's not open yet—maybe later this year. It depends on Professor Sumimoto," he needles his colleague gently. "My work is done."

"Transcribing the marginalia is slow work," Sumimoto protests over her tea.

"But you've scanned the whole thing?"

This question elicits sighs from both.

"Well," Yabuki says, "at first we took photographs of the Folio and then scanned. A lot of work. We took the photo, film went to the company, they developed it, then scanned it, then sent it to us—all very slow."

"When we began," Sumimoto explains, "they told us that for funding, we must do this on film."

"Very, very slow. And the file sizes! Each one is two hundred meg. But now we use a digital camera—much faster, and the file size is now around one-twenty, one-forty megabytes. We wanted a high-quality image for the website, so you can zoom in—see the texture, see *everything*, just like a paper book."

"And it's stored"—I motion around the room—"on these hard drives?"

"We back up onto tape," Yabuki frames a large imaginary reel with his hands.

I'm startled. Didn't that go out with platform shoes and fondue pots?

"Magnetic tape?"

"Yes, magnetic. It is very reliable. CD-ROMS, hard drives—digital media"—the computer scientist waves his hand dismissively—"I don't trust so much. They have to be backed up every—oh, ten years. Which we will do. The site is stored on tape and hard drive and CD-ROM. But magnetic tape, I trust more."

He pulls up the website in progress from their intranet, and on it, an image afloat in a black background, is the Meisei Folio, which I've just held and gazed upon. You can jump between pages and zero in on marginal notes and transcriptions of these notes. But along the side is something else, tabs reading F1, F2, F3, and F4; that is, First Folio, Second Folio, Third Folio, Fourth Folio.

"Click one," Yabuki explains, "and you go to the same page in another Folio." He picks the page of *King John* that I'd been examining back in the vault, and we instantly flash from the opening page of *King John* F1 to *King John* F2, then to F3 and F4, all seamlessly. The experience that I had just minutes ago—priceless in its rarity, and impossible for almost anyone to arrange without a screening and fifteen hours of flight—can all now happen on a computer.

To glimpse into the past in their library vault is a precious thing. But here, with the sun slanting in through the windows of Yabuki's office and playing off the screens, is something even greater: a peek into the future.

Shinjuku Metro Promenade, Tokyo

THE KEIO SEMILIMITED is rocketing Professor Yabuki and me through the amazingly endless landscape of Tokyo suburbs: miles and miles of apartments and more apartments, in shades of white and off-white concrete, all piled in parallel and perpendicular lines. The only curves come from the cars moving among them, and these are also uniformly white—it's such an immensely popular color here that one can often see Tokyo traffic jams composed entirely of white vehicles, all slowly snouting each other ahead like migrating herds of polar bears.

"This is Chōfu," Yabuki points to one sprawling tract of white concrete. "Near where I live."

"Oh, are you about to get off?"

"Normally I do. But I have an appointment at a software firm in Shinjuku this afternoon, so I will go back with you." He watches as Chōfu slips away. Its name, he explains, means "examine clothing."

"Examine clothing?"

"Yes."

The caffeine is fading out on me and the jet lag is kicking in, and I nod out with the gentle motion of the train. I notice Yabuki slumping his head into his collar, too—Examining His Clothing, I suppose. When I snap awake, the tunnels of Shinjuku have enveloped us. I pick up the conversation as if I hadn't just interrupted it with twenty solid minutes of snoring.

"I'm always curious about etymologies. What's the origin of your name?"

"Mine? *Yabuki* means"—he puffs an imaginary missile across the train—"'*blow dart.*'"

"What about your first name?"

"Ah, my uncle, Akira, was a . . . he made films? A director?"

"Really? What kind?"

"He directed many films. Have you heard of—?"

The word is lost in the roar of a passing train on the other track. I shake my head, and Yabuki mistakes my gesture; he thinks I have not heard of the film he mentioned. So he hesitantly tries again.

"He also made—a film called—*Rashomon*?"

I cut my gaze, comical with shock, from the platform to my train-mate. The salarymen arise from their seats en masse around me to disembark.

"Your uncle is . . . *Kurosawa*?"

It seems extraordinary: embodied within one family are two great evolutions of Shakespeare in Japan. In 1956, two years after *Seven Samurai* made him legendary, Kurosawa and three scriptwriters beat a retreat to a Kyoto *ryokan* lodge. They brought with them a desire to create a Japanese *Macbeth*; what they did not bring, notably, was an actual copy of *Macbeth*.

Throwing off decades of whiteface and period costumes and wigs, Kurosawa's 1957 *Throne of Blood* scarcely translates a single line from the Folio. Instead, like Shakespeare himself, Kurosawa took a powerful story and reinvented it. It was the harbinger of a generation;

Tokyo's underground Little Theatre movement would later use young actors in jeans to transpose Richard III to the scheming headmaster of a flower-arranging school, and move *A Midsummer Night's Dream* to the Forest of Arden nightclub, where the bargirls are faeries—though for the latter production, director Norio Deguchi was also memorably inspired by a Hongo bar where "the madam, who wore a black sweater, reminded me of Titania whenever she shook the cocktail shaker."

Meta-plays arose that gently spoofed the Shakespeare troupes of old, with one shown singing pathetically:

> *Shakespeare is a rice chest, a source of income.*
> *As long as he exists, we will never starve.*
> *Shakespeare is a rice granary, a substantial food source.*
> *As long as he exists, we will never die.*
> *Shakespeare has no alternate.*
> *There is no substitute for him.*

Shakespeare's words are no longer without substitute; the artists are hungry and ambitious to make his work their own. And so Kurosawa's legacy has lingered: today, one can find both a *Heavy Metal Macbeth* and traditional Shakespeare *karuta* playing cards. And, inevitably, there is now a manga *Hamlet*.

"If you want to see the latest work," Professor Yabuki suggests as we are bustled down the Keio-line platform, "you should go look in the Kinokuniya store. It's right by this station."

"That's an excellent idea," I call across the crowd.

After bidding each other farewell, Yabuki and I disappear into cross-currenting onrushes of thousands of subterranean commuters; I wander through the swirl of the Metro Promenade and into a café, where for a fixed ¥600 you can gulp down all the comics and coffee you can stand for ninety minutes. I barely make it for thirty before the desire to see more books propels me out of the café and through the station's New South Exit.

The Kinokuniya bookstore is a concrete slab of seven stories, connected by twin tendrils of pedestrian bridges off Shinjuku station's shopping complex. It's at the center of Asia's largest bookstore chain; although Kinokuniya began as a seller of lumber, by 1927 it was in the book business, and today this store embodies nearly as many stories in life as it sells in paperback. It was here, for instance, where a young jazz-club owner named Haruki Murakami once sauntered in to buy a pricey pen and a notebook set. He had, you see, decided that it might be nice to try his hand at writing a novel or something.

I cross into Kinokuniya's, and the scene that confronts me is *overwhelming*. There is no other word for it. It is a sea of brightly colored manga—shocking pinks, verdant greens, inky blacks—wildly profuse in illustration. To an American used to seeing perhaps a single manga shelf in bookstores, it is bewildering, like seeing the ocean for the first time. Framed within dark wooden shelving and piled high on tables are tens of thousands of titles, and few would give any non-native speakers a hint of what is within—*Yogurting*, or *Dollar Master*, and *What a Wonderful World!*—the latter featuring a man donning a giant teddy-bear head while running with a pistol in his hand. Even on the next floor, devoted among other things to parenting and children's books, one finds more manga—including, promisingly, a book titled *Mammoth Baby*.

In four hundred years, will someone be strolling the streets here, noting the ancient ruins, and seeking out the starting point of their most precious literature?

Manga is prolific, exuberant, crude, and often derivative, but punctuated by startling moments of brilliance—just as Elizabethan theater once was. Much is consumed here and much is carelessly thrown out, all with the easy fecundity of a golden age; but eventually some of this will be priceless, and in its own museums. To know that feeling that once was found in St. Paul's Churchyard, you could do worse than wading into the vertiginous torrents of manga in Tokyo.

The Shakespeare of the future may now be wandering the Shinjuku concourses, sketching ideas into a notebook while crammed into a subway car; time will tell. But what Kurosawa's nephew is already doing with the Shakespeare of the past raises a curious notion—one that might take many decades to realize—that someday *every* First Folio could be available to anybody. Land on a page of *Hamlet* from Tokyo, for instance, and you could instantly compare—how does it contrast with the Folio under the hammer at Sotheby's, or the Grenville and Steevens Folios in London, or with the Vincent in Washington? Or a Folio in Manchester? In Padua? In South Africa? In Los Angeles? Folios could achieve their absolute original state—of freshly inked sheets drying on lines hung over the printing press— together in one place again, no longer separated by the arbitrary combinations that shuffled them into each wandering copy.

Someday all my travels in search of the Folio may seem as quaint as the volume itself. Printed laboriously in a Barbican shop, haphazardly bound, and cast for 386 years upon the currents of chance and covetousness, Shakespeare's words are beginning to slip the bonds of mere time and place—ascending into a new life, into new lands never dreamt of in all the philosophy of their makers.

Exeunt.

FINIS.

Further Readings

Act I

For those wishing to begin the study of the First Folio, a half dozen books are a must; all other Folio commentary stands on their shoulders. The first place to start is with Peter Blayney's *The First Folio of Shakespeare* (1991); written as the brief accompanying guide to a Folger exhibition, it remains the most succinct and savvy introduction to Folio studies ever written. The genealogy of heavy-duty Folio scholarship can be traced in a straight line through R. Compton Rhodes's *Shakespeare's First Folio* (1923), Edward Willoughby's *The Printing of the First Folio of Shakespeare* (1932), W. W. Greg's *The Shakespeare First Folio* (1955), Charlton Hinman's and Peter Blayney's respective editions of *The First Folio of Shakespeare: A Norton Facsimile* (rev. 1996), and finally to the recent and Herculean labors of Anthony James West in his two volumes (and counting) of *The Shakespeare First Folio* (2001, 2003). Each of these scholars is engaged in a dialogue among themselves; each volume is vital to any serious scholar on the subject.

More on Frankfurt and its associated catalogs can be found in George Smith's article "The Frankfurt Book Mart" in volume 1 of

The Book Lover (1900), Griwoll's *Three Centuries of English Book-trade Bibliography* (1903), and Griwoll's article "The Term Catalogues and the Prototypes" in volume 1 of *The Bibliographer* (1902).

The neighborhood of St. Paul's and its booksellers are a rich vein of history, and good starting points include E. Beresford's *St. Paul's Cathedral* (1925), Edward Walford and Walter Thornbury's *Old and New London* (1878), Charles Knight's *Shadows of the Old Booksellers* (1865), and the Reverend Arthur Dimock's *The Cathedral Church of St. Paul* (1901). Some wonderful details on both the Great Fire and St. Paul's bookselling also appear in William Roberts's fine roving narrative, *The Book-Hunter in London* (1895).

Much valuable information on William Jaggard and his press came from Edwin Willoughby's *A Printer of Shakespeare: The Life and Times of William Jaggard* (1934), and in particular I drew the details about the paper used from T. C. Hansard's *Typographia: An Historical Sketch of the Origin and Progress of the Art of Printing* (1825), A. Proteaux's *Practical Guide for the Manufacture of Paper and Boards* (1866), and R. W. Sindall's *The Manufacture of Paper* (1908).

Further information on Heminge and Condell can also be found in the helpful work of Joseph Quincy Adams Jr. in his *Modern Philology* articles "William Heminge and Shakespeare" in volume 12 (May 1914) and "The Housekeepers of the Globe" in volume 17 (May 1919). Adams's 1939 reprint of *The Passionate Pilgrim* also gives useful insight into Jaggard's earliest tangle with Shakespeare's work.

More on Ben Jonson and Shakespeare's other contemporaries can be found in Martin Butler's "Jonson's Folio and the Politics of Patronage" (*Criticism*, Summer 1993), Richmond Barbour's "Jonson and the Motives of Print" (*Criticism*, Fall 1998), and John Freehafer's "Leonard Digges, Ben Jonson, and the Beginning of Shakespeare Idolatry" in volume 21 of *Shakespeare Quarterly* (Winter 1970).

A number of Folio owners have been identified for the first time in this book. The detective work involved in tracing their ownership was invigorating, if perhaps the trainspotting of literary scholarship.

And now, some locomotives.

Sir Edward Dering, the first known Folio buyer, has found a dedicated current scholar in the work of Laetitia Yeandle. I point readers in particular to her transcription of *Dering and His 'Booke of Expences': 1617–1628*, now available online at the Kent Archaeological Society. Along with the works on printers noted earlier, a colorful account of Henry Shepherd's neighborhood can be found in the notes on page 57 of Beaufoy et al.'s *A Descriptive Catalogue of the Traders, Tavern, and Coffeehouse Tokens Current in the Seventeenth Century* (1855).

Accounts of Rachel Paule (née Clitherow) can be found on page 373 of James Granger's *A Biographical History of England* (1824), as well as in a letter from James Clitherow running from pages 158 to 161 of J. P. Malcolm's edition of *Letters Between the Rev. James Granger and Many of the Most Esteemed Literary Men of His Times* (1805). A crucial proof of her book collecting can be found in her presence in Nona Labouchere's study *Ladies' Book Plates* (1895).

Sir John Hervey is duly noted in volume 4 of Collins et al.'s *Peerage of England* (1812), and Nathaniel Hawthorne notes his relation to the family in his *English Notebooks* (1855). Sir John Tonstall's story took some disentangling, though, not least because a number of John Tonstalls were running about. Accounts of his life can be found on page 38 of volume 8 of Madden et al.'s *Collectanea Topographica Et Genealogica* (1843), on page 68 of Birch et al.'s *The Court and Times of Charles the First* (1848), and on page 104 of the Reverend William Greenwell's Part II of *Wills and Registries from*

The Registry at Durham: Volume 38 of Publications of the Surtees Society (1860).

Robert Wynn of Bodysgallen Hall has perhaps the best memorial of all remaining to him: namely, the hall still stands and has been converted into a rather posh spa. To learn of the hall's premasseur-and-mud-bath era, though, you'll need to see pages 93–94 of volume 4 of the *Journal of the British Archaeological Association* (1898), Philip Yorke's *The Royal Tribes of Wales* (1799), and Wynn's entry in the *Dictionary of Welsh Biography*, now available online through the National Library of Wales.

And, of course, there's the copy that turned up at Sotheby's. Useful accounts of both Dr. Bates and Dr. Williams can be found in *Dr. Williams and His Library* (1947) and John Creary's *Dr. Williams's Library* (1977), as well as in "The Public Libraries of London" in the October 1876 issue of *American Bibliopolist*. Bates is perhaps the more interesting figure of the two, as Williams may only have acquired the Folio by accident. Personal recollections of Bates are in volume 1 of Edward Calamy's *An Historical Account of My Own Life* (1830 ed.), and useful overviews are in Robert Forman Horton's *John Howe* (1905), pages 193–94 of volume 4 of George Geoffrey Cunningham's *A History of England in the Lives of Englishmen* (1853), page 445 of volume 5 of John Stoughton's *Ecclesiastical History of England* (1874), and in the introductory memoir *The Whole Works of the Rev. W. Bates, D.D.* (rev. 1815 edition). Also, a good account of Hackney in Bates's time is in volume 2 of Henry Benjamin Wheatley's *London, Past and Present* (1891).

The Williams copy's previous owner, John Plomer, was a hard nut to crack, and I must still classify his identification as simply an educated guess. What guesswork I could make, though, is indebted to the genealogical zeal of the descendants of one of his apprentices. LeAnne Seely's article "Robert Seeley's London" in volume 16 of the *JASFO Newsletter* notes that a cordwainer named John Plomer was living in London in 1623 and that he was flush enough to take an apprentice, Robert Seely, from the town of Huntingdon. A connection between Plomer and the town is a distinct possibility; families often sent their sons to apprentice with friends or relatives. Certainly the will of one John Plomer was proved in the town of Walesley, on January 17, 1648, and can be found in volume 1 of Matthews et al.'s *Abstracts of Probate Acts in the Prerogative Courts of Canterbury* (1906). If our Plomer's estate was sold off at about this time, it would help account for the 1650s rebinding of the Folio. Without further records, though, we may never know for sure.

Finally, my coverage of Sotheby's was greatly assisted by the house's auction catalogs: *Sotheby's English Literature: History, Fine Bindings, Private Press and Children's Books, Including the First Folio of Shakespeare* (2006), and the hardbound volume they put out specifically for Lot 95—yes, it was that big of a deal—*The Shakespeare First Folio, 1623: The Dr. Williams's Library Copy* (2006).

Antiquarian catalogs, incidentally, are one of those brilliant resources that few scholars and not even many collectors ever hear about. Old Maggs Bros. catalogs, in particular, are catnip for any serious bibliophile. They're not an obvious source, granted: why read old listings from seventy and eighty years ago, for books that are no longer for sale—indeed, for copies that might have been destroyed in floods and fires years ago? Yet their descriptions are practical guides to literature, written by people who live and breathe old books, and whose very livelihood depends on their ability to describe them. They contain bursts of chance and circumstance: booksellers are

not limited by any preconceived notion of noteworthy literature, because they have to describe *whatever happens to wander in through
their front door.*

And so allow me to direct you to two wonderful old Maggs
books: the first, naturally, would be catalog #434, *Shakespeare and
Shakespeareana* (1923). But best of all is catalog #574, *Curiouser and Curiouser! Strange Books and Curious Titles* (1932), which culls all the
prime oddities from their trove of old works. My personal favorite—
a 1642 volume titled *Turn-Over and Read. And after Reading,
Censure*—was surely a snip at just £3 15s.

Act II

As a historian and a memoirist, I'm painfully aware of the very real
failings of any books written by *people who weren't there.* Clever
narrative and elisions can cover up a lot, and one can thrust pin-
pricks into the details of the actual witnesses, deflating them while
puffing up one's own revisionism. *But we weren't there.*

Yet I want to single out Don-John Dugas's *Marketing the Bard*
(2006) as worthy of particular attention: completely unadorned
with any theoretical flash and dazzle, it is quite possibly the most
useful work of Shakespeare scholarship that I've seen from the last
decade. Maybe it's the publishing wonk in me, but I found Dugas's
willingness to dive into account ledgers and the nuts and bolts of
copyright to be an incredibly useful perspective on the workings
of publishing in the eighteenth century. We need more studies like
this one: books are a business, and to understand the creation of literature also means understanding what happens between the garret
and the bookstore. Dugas makes an extensive case for the signifi-

cance of the battle between Walker and Tonson, one that convinced me to include it as a major part of my own narrative.

On a similar note, Kathleen Lynch's *Jacob Tonson, Kit-Kat Publisher* (1971) gives an invaluable account of the Tonson family's extraordinary place in London publishing during the eighteenth century. Robert Walker's distribution network is discussed in Michael Harris's *London Newspapers in the Age of Walpole* (1987), and he also figures in some of the copyright tumult in Ronan Deazley's *On the Origin of the Right to Copy* (2004).

A useful account of the task that Rowe faced is in Robert Hamm Jr.'s "Rowe's Shakespeare and the Tonson House Style" in volume 31 of *College Literature* (2004), and the broader picture also emerges from Grace Ioppolo's "The Old and New Revisionists" in volume 52 of *Huntington Library Quarterly* (1989).

A number of studies detail the battle between Alexander Pope and Lewis Theobald. So many, in fact, that I wonder whether scholars see a bit of themselves in Theobald: the hardworking library drudge, the ant to Pope's grasshopper. Thomas Lounsbury's *The Text of Shakespeare* (1906) remains useful, as does Richard Jones's *Lewis Theobald: His Contribution to English Scholarship* (1919), Peter Seary's *Lewis Theobald and the Editing of Shakespeare* (1990), Caroline Roberts's "Lewis Theobald and Theories of Editing" in *Reading Readings* (1998), edited by Joanna Gondris, and "The Birth of the Editor" in Andrew Murphy's *A Concise Companion to Shakespeare and the Text* (2007).

The public battles between Pope and Theobald also turn up in George Winchester Stone Jr.'s "Shakespeare in the Periodicals, 1700–1740" in volume 3 of *Shakespeare Quarterly* (1952). There's helpful context for Theobald's early Shakespeare-influenced work in James Sutherland's "Shakespeare's Imitators in the Eighteenth Century" in volume 28 of the *Modern Language Review* (1933).

Cardenio occupies its own rather neglected but curious corner of Shakespeare studies; one of the best recent contributions has been Howard Marchitello's "Finding *Cardenio*" in volume 74 of *ELH* (2007). Major earlier accounts include Walter Graham's "The *Cardenio Double Falshood* Problem" in volume 14 of *Modern Philology* (1916), Gamaliel Bradford Jr.'s "The History of *Cardenio* by Mr. Fletcher and Shakespeare" in volume 25 of *Modern Language Notes* (1910), and John Freehafer's "*Cardenio*, by Fletcher and Shakespeare" in volume 84 of *PMLA* (1969). Further context can be found in G. Harold Metz's *Four Plays Ascribed to Shakespeare* (1982).

For location work, there's nothing quite like old Baedekers and Hutton's *Literary Landmarks of London* (1885). For some of the specific details in this section, I found Turn-Again Lane described in volume two of Fuller and Nuttall's *History of the Worthies of England* (1840), in Wheatley's *London, Past and Present*, and as an entry in the 1907 edition of W. Carew Hazlitt's *English Proverbs and Proverbial Phrases*. Useful accounts of St. Paul's Coffee-House were in William Roberts's *The Book-Hunter in London* (1895), Henry C. Shelley's *Inns and Taverns of Old London* (1909), and Peter Ditchfield's *Memorials of Old London* (1908). The account of Ben Jonson at Gray's Inn is from a long footnote on page 415 of volume 1 of the variorum *Plays and Poems of William Shakespeare* (1821). Thornbury's *Old and New London* (1878) was also of help and, in any case, is worth reading simply for its sheer fascination.

Samuel Johnson is such an exhaustively covered author that it's tempting to say that it's hard to know where to start: tempting, but untrue. Boswell's *The Life of Samuel Johnson* is, of course, the first place to start; I found Alexander Napier's edition of 1884 helpful. Robert Anderson's *The Life of Samuel Johnson* (1815) is a good additional angle on the man, as is Hector Piozzi's *Anecdotes of Samuel Johnson* (1786).

Bruce Redford's five-volume collection, *The Letters of Samuel Johnson* (1992–94), was particularly vital in developing a chronology for Johnson, as well as getting a sense of his state of mind. Additional context is to be found in Richard B. Schwartz's *Daily Life in Johnson's London* (1983), Dorothy Marshall's *Dr. Johnson's London* (1968), and particularly in Lyle Larsen's *Dr. Johnson's Household* (1985).

The account of Bream's Buildings is from a fascinating article titled "In Difficulties: Three Stages. The First Stage: The Sponging House," which ran in the July 20, 1867, issue of *All Year Round*. The sponging house in Bream's Buildings was where new arrestees could stay in a slight degree of comfort while they appealed to their friends for money . . . hence the name. If they failed, they were packed off to the prison on Whitecross Street. Johnson noted that he wrote to Richardson from the sponging house.

Along with the above sources, the details about David Garrick were also drawn from his friend Arthur Murphy and his biography *The Life of David Garrick* (1801).

My section on Charles Burney was greatly helped by Klima et al.'s compilation of *Memoirs of Dr. Charles Burney, 1726–1769* (1988), as well as by volume 1 of Alvaro Ribiero's *The Letters of Charles Burney, 1751–1784* (1991). No second volume of Burney's letters has yet appeared, though it will be worth the wait. The felonious college career of his son Charles Jr. can be found in all its glory—with a long list of the books he stole—in J. C. T. Oates's "Charles Burney's Theft of Books at Cambridge" in volume 3 of *Transactions of the Cambridge Bibliographical Society* (1962).

At the heart of this chapter were the actual collected works of Shakespeare by Nicholas Rowe (1709), Alexander Pope (1725), Lewis Theobald (1734), William Warburton (1747), Samuel Johnson (1765), and George Steevens (1773), as was Theobald's *Shakespeare Restored*

(1726), *Double Falshood* (1728), and the various Shakespeare-related works of Samuel Johnson. The latter are collected in Wimsatt Jr.'s *Samuel Johnson on Shakespeare* (1960), more broadly in Brian Vickers's compilation *Shakespeare: The Critical Heritage* (1974), and in *Johnsonian Miscellanies* (1897), edited by George Birbeck Hill.

These editors are also covered in Simon Jarvis's *Scholars and Gentleman* (1995) and Colin Franklin's *Shakespeare Domesticated* (1991), which also gives a handy overview of the various editions of his collected works; David Scott Kastan's *Shakespeare and the Book* (2001) also provides a handy brief overview of the various editions and of the historical currents around them. Arthur Sherbo's *The Birth of Shakespeare Studies* (1968) also delves into these early editors, as does his *Samuel Johnson, Editor of Shakespeare* (1956). Surprisingly, the only book-length account of Steevens is Sherbo's *The Achievement of George Steevens* (1990).

The account of the daily rounds that Steevens made around London and of Isaac Reed's aversion to editorial recognition both come from their contemporary John Nichols; in fact, for sheer unscholarly gossip on many of the figures in this section, nothing quite tops John Nichols and his collections *Literary Anecdotes of the Eighteenth Century* (1812) and *Illustrations of the Literary History of the Eighteenth Century* (1817–58). Drawn straight from the correspondence and reminiscences of the people who were actually there, it's as close as you can get to lurking around the coffeehouses where these writers gathered. Although Nichols notes that Steevens habitually stopped by Mudge's to set his watch, the connection does not seem to have been traced further: Thomas Mudge's father was in fact the surgeon Dr. John Mudge, and his grandfather was the Reverend Zachariah Mudge; both were well-known to Johnson, as is first noted in Croker's 1835 edition of Boswell's *Life of Samuel Johnson*.

Hawthorne's account of the Staple Inn courtyard comes from his *English Note-Books* (1855), and Thomas Worsfold's *Staple Inn and Its Story* (1903) gives a fine account of the place; if you're looking to retrace steps, he notes that Reed moved in 1799 from Staple Inn No. 1 to No. 11. And while the Temple of the Muses is long gone, the proprietor's *Memoir of the First Forty-Five Years of the Life of James Lackington* (1792) is well worth reading.

My account of the Folio's leaping prices and popularity in the second half of the eighteenth century is especially indebted to Anthony James West's painstaking work in the first volume of *The Shakespeare First Folio* (2001). The heart of this section really is in Steevens's account of auctions in his 1793 edition of Shakespeare, and in three wonderful copies of auction catalogs now possessed by the British Library: *A Catalogue of the Genuine Library of the Late John Watson Reed* (1790), *Bibliotheca Steevensiana: A Catalogue of the Curious and Valuable Library of George Steevens, Esq.* (1800), and *Bibliotheca Reediana* (1807), covering Isaac Reed's library. A page from Steevens's copy of the 1790 Reed catalog is also laid into the Burney Folio. The library's full copy of that catalog, though, was owned and annotated by collector Thomas Park, who attended the auction and jotted down the buyers and the prices paid. There's also a note by Park that reveals that Roxburghe's agent got his old Folio—not a bad perk.

Act III

Tracking down Folios is a long and sometimes heartbreaking task. Each generation of Folio hunters has surely found a great many paths that led their books to fire, water, and sheer oblivion. It seems only fitting here, in talking about Anthony West's fine work in *The*

Shakespeare First Folio: The History of the Book (2001), to note one of his discoveries that is particularly poignant. The Folio known as Lee 145—it has no West number, for reasons that will become all too clear—was shipped from London in 1851 to the comic actor William Burton, a star of the American stage who was nearly as colorful as the characters he played. (He was known, for instance, to hastily stage his own guerrilla productions of rival shows the night before their opening, just to wreck his competitors.) Burton's library was broken up by auction upon his death, and his complete set of four Folios were snapped up by the great actor Edwin Forrest. He proudly displayed them in a glass case by his desk and, upon his death, included it among the decorations and artifacts for his delightfully named Edwin Forrest Home for Decayed Actors.

Alas, the sight of old thespians thoughtfully thumbing the pages of Folios was not to be: a year later, the home caught fire. When it finally closed down in 1987, nobody was quite sure where, or if, the Folios still existed. West and librarians in Philadelphia found that the Folios' remains had been mislabeled and included in a collection sent to the University of Pennsylvania—where, mournfully, they note the "ashes are encased in glass."

Accounts of the Forrest 1623 Folio may be found in volume 2 of West, as well in Steven Escar Smith's 2006 *Gazette of the Grolier Club* article "Like Loose Leaves from an Unclasped Binding." The Griswold Folio's loss is also detailed in West. Along with the various initial accounts of the sinking of the *Arctic* in the *New York Times*, a particularly useful account of the sinking and its aftermath is in John R. Stilgoe's 2003 history, *Lifeboat*, and David W. Shaw's 2003 account, *The Sea Shall Embrace Them*.

I trust Anthony's village of High Halden will survive the censure heaped upon it by G. Phillip Bevan's *Handbook to the County of*

Kent (1878), *Black's Guide to Kent* (1874), and above all by William Henry Ireland et al.'s *England's Topographer: Or, a New and Complete History of Kent* (1829). Ireland's youthful history with Shakespeare forgery is well worth reading about in its own right; and I devote a chapter to it in my book *Banvard's Folly* (2001).

I am grateful as well to the entire lineage of Folio trackers. Dibdin's *The Library Companion* (1824) is the place to start, of course; it is famously and frustratingly rambling. His *Reminiscences of a Literary Life* (1836) also gives a somewhat sketchy account of his early years, and his friend Lord Grenville may be glimpsed in William Younger Fletcher's *English Book Collectors* (1902) and John Henry Payne and Henry Foss's *Bibliotheca Grenvilliana* (1848).

Sidney Lee's *Shakespeares Comedies, Histories, & Tragedies: A Census of Extant Copies* (1902) and his *Notes & Additions to the Census of the Copies of the Shakespeare First Folio* (1906) remain fascinating works, even if superseded by West, as does Harold Otness's *The Shakespeare Folio Handbook and Census* (1990). Curiously, Lee had a particular concern with the rate at which Folios were getting bought up by Americans, and he predicted at the end of *Notes & Additions,* "Somewhere around 1915 America and Great Britain will in all likelihood each own the same number of copies—some eighty-three apiece." By around 1930, he ventured, "the existing ratio of American and British copies, sixty-two to one hundred and five, will be exactly reversed." In fact, unknown to Lee, Folger had already acquired so many Folios that what he was writing was no speculation at all: it had already happened. And who knows? In another century's time, we may be writing the same of the U.S. folios and an Asian power such as Japan, China, or Russia. A century or two more, and perhaps they, too, will be repeating Lee's lament about, let us say, Brazil.

The curious history of Folio facsimiles has not been much

written upon, but it is fortunately rather easy to get access at libraries to the three earliest versions by E. & J. Wright (1807), Lionel Booth (1864), and Howard Staunton (1866). The history of the Wrights can be gleaned from the online *Exeter Working Papers in British Book Trade History: The London Book Trade, 1775–1800*. Arthur Sherbo's *Shakespeare's Midwives: Some Neglected Shakespeareans* (1992) gives a helpful account of the Wrights' editor, Francis Douce, and the extraordinary pen-facsimilist John Harris can be found in Robert Cowton's *Memories of the British Museum* (1872). The New York Public Library's wonderful three-portrait "Lenox Folio" is first noted in the June/July 1870 issue of *American Bibliopolist*; that account also notes the difficulties in distinguishing the 1807 Wright title page from the real thing.

The British Library still has Lionel Booth's 1860 *Catalogue of Books*, and just how badly his facsimile venture was hurt by Staunton's version may be guessed by the May 7, 1866, *Times* of London classified ad noting a bulk auction of the Booth edition for remainder dealers.

Beyond Howard Staunton's *Memorials of Shakespeare* (1864) and his 1866 facsimile folio, I'm afraid most books by or about Staunton are limited to chess; but David Levy's 1975 book, *Howard Staunton: 1810–74*, spends a least a bit of time on the man himself. Some colorful anecdotes of Staunton and the London chess scene can be found in Charles Tomlinson's 1891 *British Chess Magazine* reminiscence "Simpson's Divan." The account of Staunton's departure from chess can be found in Moncure Conway's extraordinary two-volume *Autobiography* (1904). Conway's actually a key protagonist in one of my own books, *The Trouble with Tom* (2005)—the man seems to have known everyone and was a veritable Forrest Gump of the nineteenth century. Finally, Clement Mansfield Ingleby's

Shakespeare: The Book notes the importance of Staunton's facsimile, with the curious side note that the Wrights' facsimile editor, Francis Douce, was also a notable chess player—as was Ingleby himself.

Finally, I suppose that neither the most careful census nor facsimile can pick up some subtleties. Take the Boston Public Library's copy, which thanks to a careful description by bookseller Thomas Rodd in 1845 might be the Folio with the longest record of having been minutely studied. Boston's library is a maze of one marble-walled room leading to another, with no apparent order—the rare-books room, I think, is discernible by the wiring that creeps from the ceiling, its positive and negative and ground wires branching out like dangling ganglia. But there they have Folio #150, with two precious canceled leaves—these are crossed-out, uncorrected pages that were bound in—and with pages that look precisely as Rodd described them in 1845, right down to a rust spot that nailed the *1 Henry IV* line "*Prince.* It may be so;—"

Yet as I sat there, I noticed a certain . . . *barnyard aroma* in the air. I started guiltily; then I eyed the others in the room suspiciously; then I looked down at my pages in shock. Now *here* was a characteristic not noted by Rodd: a smell that wafted up with each leaf that I turned. I am not sure where this *Farting Folio* was stored in the olden days, or what substance was used to tan its binding—but I have my suspicions.

Act IV

Perhaps I have been a little hard on Folger Folio #66 to call it the *worst* one in their library; mere fragments are there, as well. In fact one other owner—at least, it would seem so—of that Folio was known. While variant spellings of the name George Gwinn led me to the entries for George Gwynn in volume 21 of *The Parliamentary or Constitution History of England* (1760), volume 1 of John Magrath's *The Flemings in Oxford* (1904), and George Cherry's *The Convention Parliament* (1966), another clue to the Folio's ownership hides in the documentation files that the Folger keeps on each of its Folios. Within the file for #66, there's an old calling card: *From the Rev. H.P. Gurney, Roseworth, Bosforth, Newcastle-on-Tyne*; on its reverse is written *Shakespeare First Folio Edition*. I would guess that the card was found inside the book itself, and that Gurney was a previous owner. The timing is right; he died in 1904, and the book was purchased from the bookseller Sotheran in 1907. A well-known mineralogist and a well-rounded author, Gurney was the principal of the Durham College of Science, which is indeed located in Newcastle-on-Tyne. Obituaries in *Geological Magazine* (February 1905) and the *Annual Register* for 1905 say that Gurney died after falling hundreds of feet in a climbing accident in Switzerland—certainly one of the more dramatic ways a Folio has changed hands.

The life of the rather more fortunate Mr. Folger can be found in Peter Blayney's *The First Folio of Shakespeare* (1991), in the funeral remembrance *Henry C. Folger: 18 June 1857–11 June 1930* (1931), and in Esther Ferington's *Infinite Variety: Exploring the Folger Shakespeare Library* (2002). Earlier accounts of Folger and his activities can also be found in A. R. Crum et al.'s *The Romance of American Petroleum and Gas* (1911) and in volume 2 of the *Biographical Record of the Alumni of Amherst College, 1821–1890* (1901). Folger's refusal to loan out his books for exhibition is singled out in "News from the Field" (p. 246) in *Public Libraries* for 1916, and photos from the early years of the Folger Library can be seen in Joseph Foster's *National Geographic* article "Biggest Little Library" (September 1951).

Tracking down the ownership of Folger #42 was the entertaining sort of goose chase that, for once, produced some actual geese. Mike Durtnall's website durtnall.org.uk, included a listing for a 1728 land-transfer document from John Elden to his family. His son Benjamin Elden's burial is noted in volume 3 of Edward Farrer's *The Church Heraldry of Norfolk* (1893). His fellow Colney resident John Brooke—the "J. Brooke" of the inscription—has a subsequent marriage to Frances Moore that is well covered indeed, given her fame as a writer. A number of accounts of Frances Moore Brooke are out there, but a useful précis of her career can be found in both the *Dictionary of National Biography* and the *Dictionary of Canadian Biography*. The Grimstons can, naturally, be found in *Burke's Peerage*, but an older account of Grimston Garth is in volume 2 of J. J. Sheahan and T. Whellan's *History and Topography of the City of York* (1857). The online Finding Aid for Grimston family records by the East Riding and Yorkshire Council also notes Florence Grimston's preserved attempt at writing a romance.

Collator technology has received a welcome wave of historical interest in the last decade, beginning with Daniel Zalewski's article "Through the Looking Glass" in the June/July 1997 issue of the late and lamented *Lingua Franca*; also, extensive accounts are in the revised edition of Richard Altick's book *The Scholar Adventurers* (1966) and in the *Studies in Bibliography* article "The Eternal Verities Verified" (2000), by Steven Escar Smith. Most recently, Joseph Dane has written further upon collation in *The Myth of Print Culture* (2003), as has Dan Gregory in "The Devil in the Details" in the July/August 2008 issue of *Fine Books and Collections*. I'm particularly thankful to Sid Berger of UC Riverside and Ian Gadd of Bath Spa University College for their e-mail correspondence with me on collation, as well as for the great generosity that Carter Hailey of the

College of William and Mary and Georgianna Ziegler of the Folger showed in demonstrating their collators. To see the fruits of collation, one need only go to Charlton Hinman's magisterial *The Printing and Proof-Reading of the First Folio of Shakespeare* (1963) and his Norton facsimile edition of the First Folio (revised by Peter Blayney in 1996).

As for Sibthorp's copy of Lee's census, I should note that in addition to the annotation on page 16, he also marked his own census entry on page 32, and just below it marked that of E. E. Harcourt Vernon, Esq.—now designated West 220. The latter is a Folio that has, intriguingly, long gone missing. The other lost Folio of this chapter, the "lottery" folio of Joseph Crisp, is noted on a raffle ticket at the Shakespeare Birthplace Trust in Stratford (Wheeler Papers, File ER 1/20). The record of Crisp's bankruptcy on November 17, 1843, is noted in volume 7, part 2, of *The Jurist* for that year.

A. B. Railton's 1899 letter recounting his discovery of the Vincent Folio is in the invaluable documentation file that the Folger keeps on Folio #1; the earliest published account is Sidney Lee's "The Shakespeare First Folio" in the April 1899 *Cornhill Magazine*. Henry Folger's own account, "A Unique First Folio," is in the November 23, 1907, issue of the *Outlook*, and *Burke's Peerage* contains useful accounts of both Augustine Vincent and the Sibthorp family. A particularly entertaining account of the old Colonel Sibthorp is in Dorothy Colville's *North Mymms: Parish and People* (1972).

As for the storied Level C, the travails in fixing its leaks are recounted in an interview with Richard J. Kuhta in "A Folger Librarian Packs Up His Books," in the Fall 2008 issue of *Folger Magazine*.

The climate in Washington doesn't help, I suppose; it was certainly instructive for me to see how a Folio might last for centuries in a library in a *dry* climate. The librarians of the University of Padua were kind enough to let me visit and see *their* First Folio. Designated West #198, it's the only First Folio known to be in Italy—and it's well hidden, as the library itself doesn't exactly announce its presence. Rather fittingly, the library is equidistant on Via San Biaggio between a publisher and a bar—up a cobblestoned street, past the students outside the Bar Rendezvous and the endless line of bicycles and scooters; past an illy café and past stenciled graffiti instructing you to ROCK ALL NIGHT; through the wooden doors, up three flights of dimly lit marble stairs and cast-iron railings, and under a crucifix into the reading room.

I examined the Folio closely while a profoundly unconcerned-looking guard nearby did sudoku. The Folio was laid flat on the desk before me, with no reading wedge to rest the book on.

No wedge?

"I have seen them at the Bodleian, but they are not for us," a staffer said, shrugging, indicating: *no budget.*

The Folio's held up pretty well, considering. It's thought this one was used by a theatrical company at some point, as a number of stage directions (*Knock* and the like) are written in the margins; it may have wound up in Padua by accompanying one of the many English students who enrolled here in the 1600s. It lay uncataloged in the library and unknown to the outside world until 1895, when its existence was announced in the July 11, 1895, issue of the *Scotsman*; since then, it's been the subject of a study by Francesco Giacobelli in his article "Shakespeare a Padova" in volume 3, no. 12, of the magazine *Padova e Il Suo Territorio* (1988).

All the leaves are still in it, but they have some remarkably crude patches made with what almost looks like white plaster; and a mouse or two may also have dined on the outer edges of the pages. To some degree, the book reflects the building that it resides in. The tables here in the reading room are perhaps a century old, maybe older, and riven with splits in the wood; just beyond them and a perimeter of 1950s metal cabinets, a line of bookcases along the outer wall sit beneath a sign affixed crookedly to the top shelf: A—BIBLIOGRAFIA. The tall windows above face a permanently blue sky, the frames surrounded by cracks; the plaster is sloughing off the wall all around the windows. There are literally chunks of fallen masonry on top of the bookshelves. They're not going anywhere anytime soon, and neither are the books; the entire effect is of a library that has been around much longer than you, thank you very much, and will still do just fine when you're gone.

Act V

It was the extraordinarily dedicated work of Akihiro Yamada at Meisei University that first fascinated me with Japan's relationship with Shakespeare. *The First Folio of Shakespeare: A Transcript of Contemporary Marginalia in a Copy of the Kodama Memorial Library of Meisei University* (1998) is a labor of love over a single Folio; I know of no other scholarly work quite like it.

My suggestion of Professor William Johnstone of the University of Aberdeen as the owner of this Meisei Folio is, I believe, the first time that the suggestion has been made, although I'm deeply indebted to the hard work of Professor Yamada for pointing me in the right direction. A brief account of William Johnstone can be found in Betty Ponting's article "Mathematics at Aberdeen," *Aberdeen University Review* 48 (1979–80): 26–35, 162–76. There's even more in an extended biographical footnote from pages 365–66 in Charles Farquhar Shand's 1845 reprint of *The Funeral Sermons, Ora-*

tions, Epitaphs, and Other Pieces on the Death of the Right Rev. Patrick Forbes, Bishop of Aberdeen (1635).

Harold Otness's "The Movement of Shakespeare Folios to Japan," *AB Bookman Weekly*, September 17, 1990, gave me some early hints about the Japanese acquisition of Folios, and I was immeasurably helped in learning more by Anthony James West, Mitsuo Nitta, and Professors Noriko Sumimoto and Michiro Yabuki. I also owe a debt of gratitude for the translations behind several of the quotes in Act V: Toshihiko Shibata for the quote from Kinoshita Junji, Yoshihara Yukari for the translation from *A World of Money*, and Kaori Ashizu for the translation of *Shakespeare's Hamlet and Its Oriental Materials*.

For those delving into Shakespeare and Japan, their first stop after the Meisei site is also online. As emblematic as *Hamlet* is to Japan's regard for Shakespeare, Kaori Ashizu's 2005 paper "What's *Hamlet* to Japan?"—online at the New Variorum Hamlet Project— may well be the best single introduction to the bard's overall history there.

The modern production of Shakespeare in Japan is well covered in *Shakespeare and the Japanese Stage* (Sasayama et al., 1999), especially in Akihikio Senda's "The Rebirth of Shakespeare in Japan" and Minoru Fujita's "Tradition and the Bunraku Adaptation of *The Tempest.*" *Shakespeare in Japan* (Kishi and Bradshaw, 2006) is particularly useful for its accounts of Shoyo and Kurosawa. Mariko Ichikawa's "Time Allowed for Exits in Shakespeare's Plays" (in Yoshiko Kawachi's *Japanese Studies in Shakespeare and His Contemporaries*, 1998) epitomized to me the extremes of painstaking Shakespeare scholarship in modern Japan, and I also found useful material in Toshihiko Shibata's "Voices and Silences in Shakespeare" (in Kishi et al.'s *Shakespeare and Cultural Traditions*, 1991).

For an analysis on the cultural significance of Shakespeare in nineteenth-century Japan, I highly recommend Yoshimara Yukari's fascinating chapter "Japan as 'Half-Civilized'" in *Performing Shakespeare in Japan* (Ryuta et al., 2001). Also see the book's coverage of prewar Shakespeare adaptations in James R. Brandon's "Shakespeare in Kabuki" and Ueda Munakata Kuniyoshi's "Some Noh Adaptations of Shakespeare in English and Japanese," as well as their rollicking interview with Norio Deguchi. Fine overviews also appear in *Shakespeare in Japan* (*Shakespeare Yearbook*, vol. 9, ed. by Anzai et al., 1998), particularly in Tetsuo Anzai's "A Century of Shakespeare in Japan" and Noriko Sumimoto's "Early Shakespeare Scholarship in Japan."

But everyone eventually winds up turning to the most modest-looking book of all: *Shakespeare in Japan: An Historical Survey*, a slim 1940 volume written by Toyoda Minoru for the Shakespeare Association of Japan. What makes this book particularly poignant is not only that Minoru is writing about early Shakespeare scholarship from living memory, but that the timing of his book is heartbreaking.

I can think of no better way to end my book than with the words by which Minoru began his:

> By the time the book was substantially ready for the printer, Japan was in the midst of the war with China; and while I was revising and amplifying my MS in the light of newly acquired material, the second Great War broke out in Europe.
>
> In this period of worldwide tribulation, when thousands of lives are being sacrificed and millions endangered, what significance, it may be asked, has such a study as this? We remember, however, that during the last Great War the annual

reports of the Shakespeare Society in Germany were not discontinued; and so as the proper problem for mankind to solve is man—and as the need of a solution has never been more urgent—, the appreciation, in any country, of a profound appreciator of life, such as Shakespeare or Goethe, may claim attention even in wartime. Is it not in mutual understanding and spiritual brotherhood that the final hope of humanity reposes?

Acknowledgments

This book would not have been possible without my wife, Jennifer—my first and best reader in all things—and my sons, Bramwell and Morgan, whose love reminds me of why I write.

Marc Thomas has, as always, been an immense help in all our family ventures; this book's dedication to him is surely long overdue. And I am grateful for the support given by my agent, Michelle Tessler, and by my editors, Kathy Belden and Colin Dickerman; their patience on this project approaches that of Jaggard himself.

I'd also like to thank the many scholars who were so generous with their time, including Anthony James West, Carter Hailey, Georgianna Ziegler, Betsy Walsh, Sid Berger, Ian Gadd, Michiro Yabuki, Noriko Sumimoto, Lavinia Prosdocimi, and Elena Saccomani. A number of booksellers and auctioneers were also particularly helpful, including Mitsuo Nitta, Peter Selley of Sotheby's, and Sara Fox of Christie's. And I am indebted to the staffs of many libraries, including those at the Folger Shakespeare Library, the British Library, the Library of Congress, the New York Public Library, the Sutro Library, Meisei University, the University of Padua, Cambridge University, the Boston Public Library, the Stratford Birthplace Memorial Trust, the University of Iowa, and Portland State University.

Finally, I'd like to thank the bookseller—his name is long forgotten, I'm afraid—who years ago sold me *the wrong book*. I was supposed to get a 1922 copy of David Garnett's *Lady into Fox*; instead, he accidentally mailed me Henry Benjamin Wheatley's 1898 guide, *Prices of Books*, which was edited by David's father, Dr. Richard Garnett. When I called the bookseller, he apologized and told me, *Eh, keep the book anyway, I don't know if anyone else wants a hundred-year-old price guide.* For no good reason, I sat down and read the entire thing and found myself utterly fascinated by a section on Dibdin's folio census—by the very notion of someone pursuing the trail of a single book. From that happy accident of reading, this book came into being.

Exit, pursued by a bear.

A NOTE ON THE AUTHOR

PAUL COLLINS is an assistant professor of English at Portland State University and the author of *Sixpence House, The Trouble with Tom, Not Even Wrong,* and *Banvard's Folly.* His work has appeared in *Smithsonian,* the *New York Times,* and *Slate.* He edits the Collins Library imprint of McSweeney's Books and appears regularly on NPR's *Weekend Edition* as the show's resident literary detective.